BROOKLYN BOTANIC GARDEN RECORD

PLANTS & GARDENS

GROUND COVERS AND VINES

This Handbook is a Special Printing of PLANTS & GARDENS, Vol. 32, No. 3

CONTENTS

Staff for this issue:
GARY L. KOLLER AND DONALD WYMAN, *Guest Editors*
FREDERICK MCGOURTY, *Editor*
MARGARET E.B. JOYNER, *Associate Editor*
and the Editorial Committee of the Brooklyn Botanic Garden
NANCY TIM, *Circulation Director*
DONALD E. MOORE, *President, Brooklyn Botanic Garden*
ELIZABETH SCHOLTZ, *Vice President, Brooklyn Botanic Garden*

Plants and Gardens, Brooklyn Botanic Garden Record (ISSN 0362-5850) is published quarterly at 1000 Washington Ave., Brooklyn, N.Y. 11225, by the **Brooklyn Botanic Garden, Inc.** Second-class postage paid at Brooklyn, N.Y., and at additional mailing offices. Subscription included in Botanic Garden membership dues ($20.00 per year), which includes newsletters, announcements and plant dividends. Separate subscription membership ($10.00) includes *Plants & Gardens* and newsletters. Copyright © 1978, 1987 by the Brooklyn Botanic Garden, Inc.

Roses come with many growth habits. Some of them are capable of being either vines or ground covers. 'Silvermoon', a hybrid climber, is shown here.

LETTER FROM THE
BROOKLYN BOTANIC GARDEN

Over the years BBG has taken a close look in print at various plant subjects, and some sixty Handbooks on different themes have appeared. One of the gaps in the series has been on ground covers, and in view of the trend toward smaller, low-maintenance gardens, a mini-manual on "living carpets" is long overdue. We are indebted to Mr. Gary Koller of the Arnold Arboretum of Harvard University for serving as guest editor of this section of the Handbook.

Vines, some of which are indeed ground covers in their own right, are discussed in another section of this Handbook. Interest in them seems to be again on the rise for a number are ideal city plants. They soften the harsh concrete corners and often just poor architecture of older buildings in a way no other kind of plant can. Many of them are rough-and-tumble growers, able to thrive under difficult growing conditions and to give beauty at little cost in money or space. We are fortunate in having a lifelong student of vines, Dr. Donald Wyman, esteemed Horticulturist Emeritus of the Arnold Arboretum, serve as guest editor of the vine section of this Handbook. In this effort he brings up to date the information on vines presented in an earlier BBG guide.

Both ground covers and vines, if properly chosen and given a modicum of care, rank with mulches as the greatest labor-savers in the contemporary garden. Before making any selections of them, however, it is wise to carefully study the attributes and limitations of particular ones. Some are rambunctious, frolicsome growers, satisfactory for only large, informal areas; others are refined, slow growers that are in place only in small gardens. It is said elsewhere in this Handbook, but the point is worth underlining—when possible, visit a nearby botanic garden or arboretum and see how the plants behave in action.

Many thanks to guest editors Koller and Wyman, and their contributors, for making this new Handbook possible. In the course of your own garden planning this year or next, include some ground covers and vines and you will be astonished how they can bring a still picture to life. No garden is complete without them.

Sincerely,

Frederick McGourty

Editor

GROUND COVERS
IN THE LANDSCAPE
William H. Frederick, Jr.

Ground covers are part of virtually every satisfying garden picture. Because there is a great variety from which to choose, they provide the potential for horticultural enrichment. Even more importantly, however, they contribute significantly to the structure and overall aesthetic strength of our gardens.

Unification

Ground covers unify the many diverse elements that occur in a single garden scheme. For instance, our exuberant tendency to grow many varieties of plants might lead us to place together in a sunny location shrubs of such varying forms as forsythia, firethorn and butterfly-bush. Tying them together with a ground cover of rock-spray cotoneaster (*C. horizontalis*) would create unity out of diversity. As another example, a grove of tulip-trees, dogwood and spice-bush, growing in a semi-shaded area, would be greatly enhanced by a ground cover of pachysandra.

Tie to the Earth

The presence of ground covers brings tree and shrub groupings into repose with the earth on which they grow. Taller covers provide the transition from trees and shrubs to lower covers and these in turn to an open-space "carpet."

In a wooded area a mass planting of cinnamon fern may provide transition from tree and shrub groupings to a carefully preserved moss patch. The moss in turn may provide the transition from the ferns to the smooth, mirror-like surface of a pond.

The same technique can apply to a sunny garden if, say, a large group of the vigorous yellow-flowered Hyperion day-lily is planted between trees and shrubs. In front, a lower, even more extensive planting might consist of *Sedum*

kamtschaticum, which has yellow-green foliage. It in turn might be used to provide transition from the day-lilies to a stone-surfaced terrace.

Dramatization of Land Contours

Any single ground cover planting is of uniform height when grown in the same exposure, and this can be a means of emphasizing land contours. If the land is level the cover will have the tranquil quality of a lake surface, an example of which is the traditional "green" on a golf course. If the land has pleasant undulations these will be dramatized by the ground cover. We see this successfully carried out in contemporary mound plantings where tight-growing covers such as *Juniperus horizontalis* 'Wiltonii' have been used.

Definition of Open Spaces

Finally, and most significantly, ground covers define shapes of open areas in our gardens. Open areas may be used for, among other things, eating, sitting or playing games. Without open spaces our gardens would be functionally useless. In addition, gardens would be dull if solidly planted, without the visual relief of occasional open spaces.

If these spaces have a strong and pleasing shape that is clearly defined, the garden is rewarding to see at all seasons of the year. It is the quality of this "leftover space" that really counts. In designing gardens this is where we should start, rather than with flower borders, screens and groups of shrubs. If the shape of the space is not satisfying, the most attractively arranged planting of trees and shrubs may fail. The shape may be curvilinear or rectilinear. In contemporary gardens this shape is often as carefully studied and proportioned as a Mondrian painting or a Matisse "cut-out" and gives

Three varieties of hosta and a dwarf yew give texture and color interest to a low border. These plants are also shade tolerant.

the viewer equal satisfaction.

Ground covers give crisp, permanent definition to these forms. It is usually appropriate to use only one ground cover in an area, and to use it in great quantity. This is, of course, a blow to the gardener who enjoys collecting many varieties of plants (and there are more ground covers to choose from than there are trees and shrubs). Restraint, however, is the key to success.

Because it provides the transition from the open space to the mass of the shrub and trees groupings, the size of the ground cover planting in this context will depend on the size of these latter two elements. It is a matter of creating a total picture of pleasing proportions.

The open space itself is most often planted in lawn grass, which is indeed a ground cover, but it may also be composed of other plant materials such as moss, heather or thyme. It may be peb-

bles, water or a paving such as flagstone, brick or blacktop. As an example, a beautiful shady, curvilinear lawn might be defined entirely by a mass planting of *Liriope muscari* 'Big Blue'. The definition, on the other hand, might be a series of three huge drifts of ground covers of different heights such as Baltic ivy (*Hedera helix* cv.), green-white variegated *Hosta* 'Thomas Hogg' and weeping English yew (*Taxus baccata* 'Repandens').

Scale, Texture and Color

We must always consider the scale or size of our gardens and select ground covers of appropriate size. Owners of city gardens may well want to think in terms of *Euonymus fortunei* 'Minima', thymes, Bowles periwinkle (*Vinca minor* 'Bowles'), sempervivums and blue fescue (*Festuca ovina glauca*), all of which are small growers. Suburbanites, with larger gardens, may prefer mass plantings of bolder materials such as *Yucca glauca, Ilex crenata* 'Helleri' and *Fothergilla gardenii.*

A landscape architect thinks of ground covers (and other plants) as tools to use in reaching design objectives. In this respect, there are both texture and color with which to work.

Ground covers with broadleaf texture such as European wild ginger (*Asarum europaeum*), *Ajuga pyramidalis* 'Metallica Crispa' and mountain cranberry (*Vaccinium vitis-idaea minus*) have distinct light-reflective qualities that remind the viewer of a water surface. Those with narrowleaf texture such as lawn grass, hay-scented fern, moss phlox, armeria and paxistima absorb light. This gives the designer the opportunity to increase light in a dull corner with broadleaf plantings and to absorb light with narrowleaf ones where the garden is bright and is used primarily in the middle of the day during the sunnier seasons of the year.

The use of color requires careful thought. The designer must consider the colors of buildings, fences and paving because they usually dominate any scene, and plants should harmonize with them.

The conscientious designer also observes the time of day and the time of

Flowers of *Ajuga reptans* show how it obtained the name "bugle." Small but heavily textured leaves give it character when not in bloom.

year the area is most frequently used. All-year use will require either evergreen ground covers, herbaceous covers which have persistent foliage (*Geranium macrorrhizum*), or deciduous kinds with attractive branching habits (*Cotoneaster horizontalis*), twig formation (*Salix repens argentea*) and/or bark color (*Vaccinium angustifolium laevifolium*). Summer-evening use may well dictate plants with a cooling effect such as *Hosta plantaginea* with its light green foliage and "fresh white" flowers.

Designing for Mood

Finally, the designer must decide what mood he is attempting to create. If the garden is to calm, soothe and bring weary minds into repose with nature, shades of green such as are found in Quaker-ladies (bluets), sweet woodruff, dwarf sarcococca and bergenia may be the key.

On the other hand, a direct assault on the tensions of today's working world may require a studied exuberance, to be provided by mass planting of ground covers with colorful foliage or flowers. There are many candidates to choose from. In a sunny situation of large scale

Lamb's ears *(Stachys byzantina)* with its downy grey-green fuzz contrasts handsomely with the granite-quartz boulder.

George Taloumis

William H. Frederick, Jr.

A short but steep bank holds its soil and form with a planting of pachysandra. Sugar maples *(Acer saccharum)* provide the shade that the ground cover requires.

one might place a drift of fountain grass *(Pennisetum alopecuroides)* in front of a mass planting of Crimson Pygmy barberry *(Berberis thunbergii* cv.). The pink-beige floral stalks of the grass would be seen against the bronzy purple-red of the barberry foliage. If space permitted, a large foreground planting of leadwort *(Cerato-stigma plumbaginoides)* with its cobalt-blue flowers would provide further enrichment.

In a smaller garden, a blue-white-yellow scheme might capitalize on inter-locking sweeps of the blue-flowered *Veronica pectinata,* the chartreuse-leaved *Thymus* x *citriodorus* 'Aureus' and the diminutive grass-like foliage of *Carex morrowii* 'Variegata' with its clearly defined longitudinal green-white leaf variegation.

If you have a hankering for grays and blues, plant lamb's ears *(Stachys byzantina)* and mouse's ears *(Cerastium tomentosum)* to provide big puddles of interlocking gray foliage for the blue grassy tufts of blue fescue *(Fescuta ovina glauca),* accented by a few clumps of the slightly larger-scale blue oat *(Helicto-*

trichon sempervirens).

Just as much exuberance can occur in shady situations. Again, if your preference is for grays and blues, plant a few clumps of the dramatic large blue-leaf *Hosta sieboldiana* amid interlocking drifts of the Japanese painted fern *(Athyrium nipponicum* 'Pictum'), variegated gout-weed *(Aegopodium podagraria* 'Variegatum') and *Pachysandra terminalis* 'Variegata'.

Chartreuse colorations are stimulating where shadows are deep. Here one can have fun with *Hosta* 'Frances Williams', *H. lancifolia* 'Kabitan' and *Liriope muscari* 'Variegata' and, if there is enough light, Buttercup or Goldheart ivies *(Hedera helix* cvs.).

Selecting the most appropriate ground covers is as exacting a challenge as planning the menu for a gourmet meal. We must be aware not only of the merits of each course (or each plant), but also sensitive to their aesthetic relationship to each other. Most importantly, we must exercise restraint and selectivity among an overwhelming array of tempting possibilities. ❧

7

For extra rewards give attention to the . . .

PLANTING AND CARE OF GROUND COVERS

Mervin C. Eisel

In addition to the beauty they provide, ground covers can accomplish several useful functions in the landscape. Among the most important are soil stabilization and low maintenance. Ground covers can serve as a unifying element in a landscape design. The taller kinds can be used to create masses that balance architectural features. On a slope, dense-growing ground covers will prevent erosion, a very important function.

Many gardeners have the mistaken idea that ground covers need little or no maintenance, but properly used they can reduce work in the yard. The care required is largely dependent on how well the plants are adapted to the microclimate and soil of the site. If the proper plants are not selected, no other garden area, including the flower borders, will require more maintenance to keep in presentable condition.

Weeding and Spacing

Tall perennial grasses, such as quack, brome and reed canary, are menaces in low, refined ground covers. Eradicating them and other weeds prior to planting is essential. Even then it takes constant vigilance to prevent the area from becoming invaded by weeds. Hand hoeing or pulling to remove weed seedlings is one of the most successful methods. In some cases the careful use of the proper pre-emergent herbicides can reduce the amount of hand weeding required.

Ideal ground covers are those that are dense or vigorous enough to shade out competitors. Also, a plant adapted to the site and which grows strongly is more likely to hold its own than one that is barely able to stay alive. Even with the most vigorous ground covers some nursing in the form of hand weeding, hoeing, mulching or the use of herbicides may be necessary to get them established. Herbaceous plants as well as shrubs that spread by rhizomes or roots where the stems touch the soil are often more competitive than others. Where aesthetic considerations permit, a more practical approach is to select a ground cover that outgrows its potential competition.

The initial spacing of plants has a great effect on the rate at which the ground cover fills an area and is able to hold its own. The sooner the ground is covered, the less likelihood undesirable plants will become established. A good rule of thumb for spacing is about one foot on center for vigorous herbaceous plants and 4" to 8" for slow-growing species.

The decision of spacing or size of plants used is often based on what a person can afford. It is often a trade-off between higher initial maintenance for wide spacing or less maintenance for close spacing. The spacing might be dependent on how large an area is to be planted. Most homeowners can afford a close spacing if only a small planting site is involved. The spacing of shrubs should be as close as two to three feet depending on the ultimate size of the shrubs, or even a one-foot spacing for dwarf shrubs.

There are few low-growing ground covers that are aggressive enough to hold their own without assistance from the gardener. Carpeting junipers are a prime example. They are attractive and hold the soil but in many plantings become badly infested with weeds unless the gardener is on watch. Japanese garden juniper (*Juniperus procumbens*) and Skandia Juniper (*Junipera sabina* 'Skandia') are two of the most competitive of the low-growing kinds. In many situations the taller spreading junipers can hold their own, provided they are resistant to juniper blight. This disease causes the foliage to become sparse, allowing weeds to come through.

Dense, mounding texture and good winter color make *Juniperus squamata* 'Prostrata' an excellent dwarf ground cover.

Some broad-leaved evergreens, deciduous shrubs and vines are effective as taller ground covers. They include hedge cotoneaster (*Cotoneaster lucidus*), Emerald Mound honeysuckle (*Lonicera xylosteum nanum cv)*, bush-honeysuckle (*Diervilla lonicera*), gray dogwood (*Cornus racemosa*), shrubby potentilla *(Potentilla fruticosa),* American bittersweet (*Celastrus scandens*) and sumacs (*Rhus glabra, R. aromatica* and *R. trilobata*). Sumacs are good examples of ground covers that cope with competition, growing above grasses and weeds and concealing them so the area does not appear unkempt. These grasses and weeds survive and prevent soil erosion. In fact, some grasses are among the best ground covers, and may be left unmowed if the area is informal.

Many of the herbaceous ground covers that are sun tolerant are not able to hold their own against weeds. Two that can, but without refined appearance, are fleeceflower (*Polygonatum cuspidatum compactum*) and crown-vetch (*Coronilla varia*). Because of their aggressiveness they often invade other garden areas, so care should be taken to curtail their spread outside the area designated for their cultivation.

Shade

Shade is a problem to be contended with on many sites because pests and weeds are usually different from those encountered in sunny areas. There are many shade-tolerant herbaceous plants, however, so lack of light is usually not in itself a major problem. More apt to cause difficulties is the competition from large shallow-rooted trees that take water and nutrients from the soil. For this reason, shade from architectural structures is easier to contend with than shade from trees. One solution may be to remove trees that are overcrowded or in poor condition.

Among the plants best adapted for shade are plantain-lilies (*Hosta*), lily-of-the-valley, violets, Jacob's-ladder (*Polemonium caeruleum*), Mayapple (*Podophyllum peltatum*) and goutweed (*Aegopodium podagraria*). Although they are rugged, an annual application of fertilizer in early spring is usually beneficial.

For the sake of uniformity many home owners attempt to grow the same ground cover in both sunny and shady locations. There are few plants that are adapted to such environmental extremes, so it is usually necessary to use different plants. Areas that receive partial shade might have still another kind of ground cover. In such cases when different plants are used in close proximity thought should be given to texture and color harmony.

The amount of light in winter deserves

9

Mervin C. Eisel

Honeysuckle 'Emerald Mound', a newer cultivar, is well suited as a ground cover because of its low, spreading habit.

consideration, too. In cooler parts of the country broad-leaved evergreen ground covers must be protected from the winter sun to prevent severe browning. Planting them only on the north side of buildings or in other shaded areas is a practical approach. On exposed sites they must have winter mulch or good snow cover, otherwise they are likely to be badly injured. Since some regions cannot depend on snow cover in the winter, other ground-cover choices, including plants that die back to the ground, or low deciduous shrubs, may be more satisfactory.

Planting on a site shaded by large trees usually results in failure unless the soil is prepared ahead of time. If this is not possible, a mulch of wood chips or other material might be a better solution than planting ground covers. (In fact, where there are many large tree roots near the surface, it might be the only solution.)

Before planting under trees, a generous layer of organic matter plus fertilizer should be deeply tilled into the soil. The tilling not only incorporates the organic matter and fertilizer, but severs some of the smaller tree roots. After the area has been planted, regular watering is usually necessary. Ideally, the site should be reworked every two or three years. While this isn't possible with perennial ground covers, at least the initial soil preparation assists in their establishment.

Salt accumulation along a roadside can be injurious to many plants. With the exception of day-lilies (*Hemerocallis*), bird's-foot trefoil (*Lotus corniculatus*) and sweet-fern (*Comptonia peregrina*), few ground covers are salt-tolerant. Ground covers such as bearberry (*Arctostaphylos uva-ursi*), sweet-fern and trailing arbutus (*Epigaea repens*) require an acid soil. Crown vetch (*Coronilla varia*) and many other legumes do better on more alkaline soil. Fortunately, most plants are adapted to a wide pH range, but it is something that should be considered before investing large sums of money or work in a ground-cover planting. The winter hardiness of plants must also be considered. Some ground covers may be tender or of borderline hardiness in your climate. They may be injured by winter and not fully recover until autumn, when the injury cycle is repeated.

At least four places come to mind where a person interested in ground covers should check for the hardiness and adaptability of different kinds of ground covers. They are your neighbors, your local nurseryman, the closest botanic garden or arboretum and your county agricultural extension agent. Most extension offices have printed horticultural information available on not just ground covers but on most areas of home garden interest. They are well worth contacting. ❧

Reflections of an Old
Pachysandra Planter

Apart from lawn grass, probably the most common ground cover in the cooler parts of the United States is Japanese spurge (*Pachysandra terminalis*). Devoting a large area to this shade-loving evergreen can be expensive if you don't already have an existing patch, especially if you want to set plants closely for fairly quick cover. About three years are needed for pachysandra to fill in completely if planted 12 inches apart.

If you have a dense bed of pachysandra and want to give over another area to it, there are few plants simpler to propagate by division. This can be done almost any time of year, but early spring is ideal because there is an entire growing season ahead for plants to become fully established. All that is needed is a sharp spade or trowel and scissors.

Pachysandra increases by stolons, in this case horizontal stems just below ground surface that give rise to new plants at the tips. Dig up a very small area and shake the soil away, and you will be amazed at the appearance—uncut subterranean spaghetti with numerous leafy shoots attached. Each one makes a new plant if severed with a piece of stolon. An existing bed of pachysandra can supply a new planting area at least fifteen times its size.

Replanting techniques vary, although none seems to fail. One of the most successful is to make a 3″ trench and insert the divisions every few inches along it. Another is to mold a little jelly roll of stolons and plant them in individual holes. We know one gardener, a frustrated sailor, who delights in tying the stolons in loose square knots. Regardless of method, the top several inches of soil should be well prepared ahead of time, preferably by the incorporation of sand and peat moss (or leaf mold, but not compost in which there is weed seed). This provides a loose, moisture-retentive medium which will encourage the spread of new stolons. An occasional application of a weakly diluted soluble fertilizer helps speed the cover. The main need the first year is watering and mulching.

A friend who works at the landscape trade reports that he asks his clients if they would like their pachysandra plants trimmed in late spring or summer to make them more "compact." His main objective, of course, is to get cuttings, which root as easily as ivy. He plants the cuttings in flats containing a mixture of half sand and half peat moss and sets them in a shady spot, where they are watered frequently. In a few weeks nearly one hundred per cent have rooted and are ready for transplanting. ✄

A wide variety of . . .

GROUND COVERS
FOR MOST REGIONS
Gary L. Koller

The term ground cover can be interpreted in many ways but it usually refers to any plant which is low, dense, persistent and easy to maintain. In addition, it should be somewhat aggressive and effective in suppressing most weed growth. The best ground covers are often little more than well-utilized weeds themselves.

Since we constantly need to evaluate plants as potential ground covers, several little-known and little-used kinds have been included which display all the desirable attributes. These are marked with an asterisk (*) and are meant only for the adventuresome. The remaining plants listed are proven performers in the milder parts of Canada and most of the United States, except for the very warmest and coldest regions. Selecting plants to fit your conditions of sun or shade, wet or dry, barren or highly organic soils and temperature extremes should equip you with a perfect candidate, and one which with the least effort, should reward you with years of beauty and pleasure.

Ajuga reptans   CARPET BUGLE
HEIGHT: 2-4 inches (5-10 cm.)
ENVIRONMENT: light shade; tolerant of full sun if watered in dry periods.
ZONE: 4; mostly evergreen in mild climates, mostly deciduous elsewhere.
ASSETS: valued for white, blue or pink flowers in May or June; foliage which may be green, purple, variegated or crinkled depending on the cultivar selected. Excellent underplanting for shrubs.
LIMITATIONS: tends to die out in spots, requiring periodic renewal planting; unless a barrier is provided it will escape into lawn areas; variegated forms tend to lack vigor.
PROPAGATION: division.

Alchemilla vulgaris *   LADY'S MANTLE
HEIGHT: 12-18 inches (30-45 cm.)
ENVIRONMENT: full sun to light shade; best growth in well-drained, highly organic soils.
ZONE: 3; deciduous.
ASSETS: attractive pleated leaves capture and highlight beads of dew or rain water; arching sprays of yellow-green flowers in May, useful in flower arrangements.
LIMITATIONS: in dry soils and intense summer heat the foliage loses its attractiveness in late summer; foliage somewhat coarse and flowers floppy.
PROPAGATION: seeds; division in spring.

Arctostaphylos uva-ursi   BEARBERRY
HEIGHT: 4-5 inches (10-13 cm.)
ENVIRONMENT: sun to light shade; tolerant of poor, sandy soils and seashore exposure; benefits from occasional application of an acid balanced fertilizer.
ZONE: 2; evergreen.
ASSETS: valued for its evergreen foliage which turns reddish-purple in the autumn, red berries are eaten by wildlife; one of the hardiest woody ground covers.
LIMITATIONS: does not transplant well, so buy container-grown plants; it must have a very acid soil (pH 5 or lower) or it will not be dense and vigorous.
PROPAGATION: cuttings taken July-September.

Aristolochia clematitis *   COMMON BIRTHWORT
HEIGHT: 24-30 inches (60-75 cm.)
ENVIRONMENT: sun to light shade; adaptable to various soils.
ZONE: 4; deciduous.
ASSETS: valued for leathery, heart-shaped leaves, borne on upright stems; small yellow flowers in July-August. Excellent for difficult banks, urban areas and seashore conditions.
LIMITATIONS: rampant; next to impossible to eradicate once established.
PROPAGATION: seeds (available from J. L. Hudson, Seedsman, Box 1058, Redwood City, Ca. 94064 U.S.A.); root pieces.

Convallaria majalis   LILY-OF-THE-VALLEY
HEIGHT: 8 inches (20 cm.)
ENVIRONMENT: sun to dense shade; best growth occurs on soils enriched with organic matter; it is a heavy feeder and benefits from periodic applications of fertilizer.
ZONE: 2; deciduous.
ASSETS: valued for upright clusters of fragrant white or pink flowers in May; excellent for difficult shady areas; dense, persistent, dependable.
LIMITATIONS: slow to get started upon transplanting; once established it may be invasive; foliage may become yellow in late summer;

Gary L. Koller

Lily-of-the-valley and sweet woodruff are mixed for contrast of foliage and texture.

fruit, which is a deep, rich orange but is seldom formed, contains a toxic substance.
PROPAGATION: division.

Cotoneaster apiculatus CRANBERRY COTONEASTER
HEIGHT: 1-2 feet (30-60 cm.)
ENVIRONMENT: full sun; well-drained soil.
ZONE: 4; deciduous.
ASSETS: valued for reddish-purple autumn foliage and abundant large red berries which remain attractive into midwinter; forms dense mounds which, when grouped, give an undulating surface effect to the mass.
LIMITATIONS: not tolerant of shade.
PROPAGATION: cuttings taken in July-August.

C. dammeri 'Skogholm'
HEIGHT: 12-15 inches (30-38 cm.)
ENVIRONMENT: full sun to light shade; well-drained soil.
ZONE: 5; evergreen.
ASSETS: vigorous; forms a dense, fine-textured mat; persistent red fruits; excellent for bank plantings; tolerant of salt spray.
LIMITATIONS: thin and lacking vigor in dense shade and heavy soils.
PROPAGATION: cuttings in August-January.

C. 'Herbstfeuer' FALL FIRE COTONEASTER
HEIGHT: 12-18 inches (30-46 cm.)
ENVIRONMENT: full sun to light shade; well-drained soil.

ZONE: 6; evergreen.
ASSETS: valued for evergreen foliage which turns maroon in the autumn and for clusters of scarlet berries which remain through winter; it spreads rapidly and roots wherever branches touch moist soil; adapted to large areas.
LIMITATIONS: growth tends to be thin and open, so dense plantings are needed for quick effect; texture is coarse and difficult to use effectively.
PROPAGATION: cuttings taken in August-January.

C. horizontalis ROCK SPRAY COTONEASTER
HEIGHT: 2-3 feet (60-90 cm.)
ENVIRONMENT: full sun; well-drained soil.
ZONE: 5; semi-evergreen in the south; deciduous in the north.
ASSETS: a spreading plant valued for reddish-purple autumn color, a herringbone branch pattern and persistent, small red berries.
LIMITATIONS: large and wide-spreading; untidy in appearance as it gets older and requires rejuvenation pruning; susceptible to scale and red spiders. Not tolerant of shade.
PROPAGATION: cuttings in July-August.

Epimedium sp. BARRENWORT, BISHOP'S-HAT
HEIGHT: 6-10 inches (15-25 cm.)
ENVIRONMENT: light to moderate shade; sun if watered during drought.
ZONE: 3; deciduous.
ASSETS: valued for delicate foliage coloration as

13

Epimedium is dense and persistent and, while generally overlooked as a ground cover, performs dependably, even under maple trees.

the new leaves unfold in spring; loose sprays of white, yellow, pink or red flowers in May; several forms have bronze autumn foliage; dense, persistent, adaptable.

LIMITATIONS: there is confusion in the nomenclature of this genus, so plants are best seen in flower before purchase; persistent foliage should be pruned away before new growth begins.

PROPAGATION: division.

Euonymus fortunei WINTERCREEPER
HEIGHT: 4-12 inches (10-30 cm.)
ENVIRONMENT: sun to dense shade; tolerant of poor soils.
ZONE: 4; evergreen or nearly so.
ASSETS: many selections are available with small leaves and low growth habit, as well as cultivars with green or variegated foliage and forms which turn purple in autumn; branches root wherever they touch soil; valuable because of its vigor and adaptability. Excellent on banks.
LIMITATIONS: the more vigorous forms climb up and over companion plants; very susceptible to scale insects which cause it to decline and die out; needs to be cut back frequently to maintain a neat appearance.
PROPAGATION: rooted layers; cuttings in July-August.

Galium odoratum SWEET WOODRUFF
(Asperula odorata)
HEIGHT: 8 inches (20 cm.)
ENVIRONMENT: light to dense shade; moist, organic soil.
ZONE: 4; deciduous.
ASSETS: valued for its fine-textured, light green foliage; for clusters of small white, star-shaped flowers in May and June; persistent and dependable.
LIMITATIONS: once established it can be invasive.
PROPAGATION: division.

Geranium dalmaticum *
HEIGHT: 4-6 inches (10-15 cm.)
ENVIRONMENT: sun to light shade; best growth in soils rich in organic matter.
ZONE: 4?; deciduous.
ASSETS: spreads rapidly by stolons; rose-colored flowers in early summer; autumn foliage tints of yellow to red.
LIMITATIONS: intolerant of drought; in some situations it may become invasive.
PROPAGATION: seed; division.

Hedera helix ENGLISH IVY
HEIGHT: 8-10 inches (20-25 cm.) as a ground cover; it is also a climbing vine.
ENVIRONMENT: sun to dense shade; in northern areas it performs best with light shade and

Hemerocallis used as a tall ground cover along a path in the Boerner Botanical Gardens, Hales Corners, Wisconsin.

shelter from sweeping winds.

Zone: 5; evergreen.

Assets: dark green lustrous foliage which is attractive year round; one of nature's most adaptable plants as to soil, exposure and ease of culture.

Limitations: in northern areas select hardy cultivars adaptable to the area; some have a yellow-green color; will climb into and over neighboring trees, shrubs, fences and walkways if not restrained.

Propagation: rooted layers; cuttings in July-September.

Hemerocallis spp. DAY-LILY

Height: foliage varies from 6 inches to 3 feet (15-90 cm.); flowering scapes vary in height depending on cultivar selected.

Environment: full sun to light shade; thrive in wet and dry soils, acid or alkaline.

Zone: 3; deciduous. Some cultivars are evergreen in South.

Assets: persistent, dependable and virtually indestructible; varietal selection allows various heights and continuous bloom sequence from early to late summer; excellent color forms available; new foliage appears early in spring. Various parts of the plant can be eaten.

Limitations: foliage may look poor in late summer. A thought should be given to landscape uses because *Hemerocallis* is routinely consigned to difficult sites, where it may not show up to best advantage.

Propagation: division.

Hosta spp. PLANTAIN-LILY

Height: 4 inches to 2 feet (10-60 cm.) depending on variety.

Environment: sun to moderate shade; water during drought; adaptable to a wide variety of soils.

Zone: 3; deciduous.

Assets: a wide selection of cultivars allows one to select for leaf shape and texture, flower color and flowering period; foliage color varies from green to blue-green and variegated and allows design flexibility. Useful for creating bold landscape effects; persistent, dependable and adaptable.

Limitations: not tolerant of drought (the foliage wilts); slugs are fond of foliage; seedlings can become weeds; on large-leaved forms the foliage may become tattered by storms and mechanical damage; new growth is rather late in the spring; much confusion in nomenclature, so plants are best seen before purchase.

Propagation: division; seeds can be used, but they will not reproduce true to type.

Juniperus chinensis sargentii SARGENT JUNIPER

Height: 12 to 18 inches (30-46 cm.); spreads 6-8 feet (2-2.5 m.)

Environment: full sun; well-drained soil.

Zone: 4; evergreen.

Assets: forms a low, dense spreading mat; adaptable to poor dry soils and the seashore; vigorous grower.

Limitations: susceptible to red spiders; not tolerant of shade.

Propagation: cuttings taken November-January.

J. conferta SHORE JUNIPER

Height: 12-15 inches (30-38 cm.); spreads 5-7 feet (2m.)

Environment: sun; well-drained soil.

Hosta varieties mixed with
low shrubs and herbs give
color interest and a unifying
texture to a border.

ZONE: 5; evergreen.

ASSETS: tolerant of exposure to spray from highway deicing salts or the seacoast; forms a dense mat; drought tolerant; selections available for increased vigor and improved winter color.

LIMITATIONS: subject to rodent damage in winter; difficult to transplant, so purchase container-grown specimens; not tolerant of shade.

PROPAGATION: cuttings taken November-January.

J. horizontalis   CREEPING JUNIPER
HEIGHT: 4 inches to 2 feet (10-60 cm.) depending on cultivar.

ENVIRONMENT: sun; well drained soil. (If grown in the shade these plants have thin foliage, lack vigor and have poor color.)

ZONE: 2; evergreen.

ASSETS: hardy for most northern areas; the wide range of cultivars available allow selection based on height, foliage color and texture. Some forms take on winter foliage coloration different from summer color. When well grown they form a dense, persistent carpet. Drought tolerant.

LIMITATIONS: initial purchase price expensive; difficult to transplant, so purchase container-grown stock; occasionally subject to red spiders.

PROPAGATION: cuttings taken November-January.

Lamiastrum galeobdolon 'Variegatum'
SILVER FROST LAMIUM
HEIGHT: 8-12 inches (20-30 cm.)

ENVIRONMENT: light shade; well-drained soil rich in organic matter.

ZONE: 4; deciduous.

ASSETS: small yellow flowers in May; the variegated foliage brightens dark shady areas; vigorous, persistent, dependable.

LIMITATIONS: intolerant of drought; invasive once established.

PROPAGATION: division in spring.

Liriope muscari   BIG BLUE LILY-TURF
HEIGHT: 12-18 inches (30-40 cm.)

ENVIRONMENT: sun to dense shade; in northern areas best growth occurs in sheltered positions.

ZONE: 6; evergreen.

ASSETS: various cultivars have been selected for flower color, vigor and foliage coloration. Tolerant of dense shade and drought. Foliage texture and color can be used to create landscape patterns. One of the best ground covers for mild climates. Terminal flowering spikes appear in July and August and range from blue to white to pink depending on cultivar.

LIMITATIONS: slugs are partial to foliage, which is eaten in strips; foliage may look shabby in winter; old leaves should be mowed prior to new growth in spring.

PROPAGATION: division.

L. spicata   CREEPING LILY-TURF
HEIGHT: 10 inches (25 cm.)

ENVIRONMENT: sun to dense shade; adaptable to a wide variety of soils.

ZONE: 6; evergreen.

ASSETS: Tolerant of drought; forms a thick, dense carpet which has the appearance of a tall, coarse lawn grass; summer foliage color is dark green; persistent and dependable.

LIMITATIONS: in northern areas winter color may be a pale green-yellow; foliage may become damaged by winter weather but the leaves can be cut back before new growth begins; slugs are fond of leaves.

PROPAGATION: division.

Ophiopogon japonicus　　MONDO-GRASS
HEIGHT: 6-10 inches (15-25 cm.)

ENVIRONMENT: sun to dense shade; best growth occurs in a moist soil, high in organic matter.

ZONE: 6; evergreen.

ASSETS: quickly forms a dense sod with dark green foliage which is slug resistant; drought tolerant; one of the easiest ground covers to maintain over time.

LIMITATIONS: in northern areas foliage may suffer winter damage.

PROPAGATION: division.

Pachysandra terminalis　　JAPANESE SPURGE
HEIGHT: 6 inches (15 cm.)

ENVIRONMENT: light to dense shade; thrives in soils which range from gravelly and well-drained to those high in clay content.

ZONE: 4; evergreen.

ASSETS: one of the most successful ground covers; it forms an evenly low mat of lush, dark green foliage; a variegated form is less vigorous but useful to add variation to plantings.

LIMITATIONS: not tolerant of full sun or drought, under which conditions it lacks vigor and the foliage becomes a sickly yellow.

PROPAGATION: division; cuttings in July-August.

Phalaris arundinacea picta　　RIBBON GRASS
HEIGHT: 2-2½ feet (60-75 cm.)

ENVIRONMENT: full sun; thrives in poor gravelly soils or moist soils.

ZONE: 3; deciduous.

ASSETS: long linear leaves with white to cream-colored stripes; excellent for dry sunny banks; spreads rapidly once established; excellent for height, textural and color contrast.

LIMITATIONS: thin and floppy in the shade; invasive, so a barrier is needed to separate it from adjoining plants; wind storms may snap the tall stems.

PROPAGATION: division.

Pulmonaria saccharata　　BETHLEHEM-SAGE
HEIGHT: 6-18 inches (15-46 cm.)

ENVIRONMENT: light to moderate shade; prefers a moist, organic soil.

ZONE: 4; evergreen or nearly so.

ASSETS: tubular flowers early in spring with colors ranging from purplish to pink and blue depending on the cultivar; white spotted leaves give a light and cheerful aspect to shaded areas all summer.

LIMITATIONS: intolerant of drought; dense colonies need to be thinned occasionally to maintain vigor.

PROPAGATION: division; seed will give a variety of floral types.

Sedum reflexum *　　JENNY STONECROP
HEIGHT: 8-10 inches (20-25 cm.)

ENVIRONMENT: sun; well-drained soil.

ZONE: 3; evergreen.

ASSETS: attractive blue-gray foliage; golden yellow flowers in midsummer; forms a dense,

George Taloumis

Shrubs and bulbs are underplanted with mondo-grass *(Ophiopogon japonicus)* for slightly coarse but pleasing evergreen texture and color. Popular in California and the South.

George Taloumis

The white-spotted leaves of Bethlehem-sage *(Pulmonaria saccharata)* will light up shaded corners much of the year.

strong-growing mat; can be used to create landscape patterns; tolerant of drought.

LIMITATIONS: flower stalks should be removed as soon as blossoms fade for seed production results in a loss of vigor and thinning of the plantings.

PROPAGATION: division; unrooted stem pieces set into new locations.

S. spurium 'Dragon's Blood'
TWO-ROW STONECROP
HEIGHT: 4-6 inches (10-15 cm.)
ENVIRONMENT: full sun to light shade; well-drained soil.
ZONE: 3; evergreen.

ASSETS: foliage occurs as bronze rosettes at the ends of short stems; red flowers in summer; drought tolerant; excellent for creating landscape patterns; this plant is one of the best carpet formers.

LIMITATIONS: foliage color fades and density thins out in moderate to dense shade.

PROPAGATION: division; stem cuttings in July-August.

Vancouveria hexandra * AMERICAN BARRENWORT
HEIGHT: 8-18 inches (20-46 cm.)
ENVIRONMENT: light to moderate shade; best growth in a highly organic soil.
ZONE: 5; deciduous.

A handsome tall ground cover or border plant, *Sedum* 'Autumn Joy' has dusty-green leaves and muted-rose flowers that deepen with age.

M. Joyner

18

Gary L. Koller

Vancouveria forms a dense, fine-textured carpet in shade. Early summer flower sprays are white.

ASSETS: forms a dense carpet of delicate compound foliage; graceful sprays of small white flowers in early summer; once established, it is vigorous and permanent.
LIMITATIONS: slow to reestablish upon transplanting; intolerant of drought.
PROPAGATION: division.

Vinca minor   PERIWINKLE, MYRTLE
HEIGHT: 6 inches (15 cm.)
ENVIRONMENT: sun to moderate shade.
ZONE: 4; evergreen.
ASSETS: one of the best evergreen ground covers; adaptable to a wide range of light and soil conditions. Floral color varies from blue to purple to white, single and double, all dependent on cultivar selected; variegated foliage forms are useful in creating landscape patterns.
LIMITATIONS: slow to get established upon transplanting; in some areas subject to a stem blight which causes dieback and thinning, giving a spotty appearance and allowing the growth of weeds.
PROPAGATION: division. ❧

Living Mulch

Many ground covers take two or three years to carpet an area completely. In the meantime weeds creep in, smothering and sometimes killing the cover. Gardeners cope in various ways—dense planting and regular fertilizing, careful application of a pre-emergence herbicide (*e.g.,* Treflan) before planting time to prevent the germination of annual weeds, and mulching with pine needles, wood chips or similar materials. But, there is still another approach.

Realizing that something is going to grow on bare soil between the ground cover plants, why not introduce plants you like? Consider interplanting ground covers in sunny areas with compatible annuals such as marigolds, zinnias and cockscomb (*Celosia*) or a vegetable crop such as radishes, lettuce, beans or tomatoes. In light shade, coleus, flowering tobacco (*Nicotiana*), begonias or wishbone flower (*Torenia*) create color, while vegetable crops can include lettuce, parsley or Swiss chard. Direct seeding between the ground cover plants allows inexpensive planting for large areas. Any surplus which develops can be considered as weed growth and pulled out.

In watering these annuals, you will also supply water to encourage better growth of the permanent ground cover planting. Frost will remove the annual flowers and vegetables so that they will not become a weed problem in themselves.

When using annuals as a living mulch, several points must be considered. First, annuals cannot be directly seeded into areas treated with pre-emergence herbicides, for the annual seeds will not germinate. Second, the annuals should not be so dense as to shade or crowd out the permanent plants, nor should they impose severe competition for water and mineral nutrients. Third, as the ground cover plants enlarge and develop, fewer and fewer annuals can be introduced without disturbing the well-being of the permanent plantings.

—Gary L. Koller ❧

19

Out-of-the-ordinary . . .

GROUND COVERS FOR VARIETY
Andre Viette

We are all familiar with the common ground covers such as ivy, pachysandra and vinca. In recent years emphasis has also been given to hosta, liriope, ajuga and dwarf ornamental grasses. Each could be the subject of an article by itself, especially in view of the many varieties available with different growth habits and floral and foliage forms.

Here is a list of fourteen plants of unique value that should be used more often as ground covers. A judicious selection, based on landscape and cultural considerations should add interest and diversity to any garden. In general, these plants are surprisingly easy to grow and maintain. The hardiness zones (Arnold Arboretum map, inside back cover) given are approximate since they will vary according to location, wind, exposure, soil, protection, sun and moisture—even within a single garden.

Asarum europaeum
Zone 4
Propagation: Division

EUROPEAN WILD-GINGER
Evergreen
Exposure: Shade

This has very attractive, round, glossy green leaves and grows to a height of 5″. It performs well under trees and shrubs, especially rhododendrons, and may self-sow in time. The small, urn-shaped flowers, which are hidden by the leaves, are greenish, purple or brown. Grown mainly for foliage.

Astilbe chinensis pumila
Zone 5
Propagation: Division

DWARF CREEPING ASTILBE
Deciduous
Exposure: Light shade or
    sun if kept moist

One of the few astilbes with a creeping growth habit. The light green foliage, which is not glossy, forms an 8″-high mat. Lavender-rose flowers appear in July or August, later than most astilbes, and are borne on spire-like stalks about 15″ tall.

Athyrium nipponicum 'Pictum'
Zone 6
Propagation: Division or spores

JAPANESE PAINTED FERN
Deciduous
Exposure: Light shade to shade

Truly a gem. There are many forms of Japanese painted fern and all are unique because of their variegated foliage. They range in height from 6″ to 18″ and leaves vary in color combinations of silver, purple, cream, green, bluish-green and gray. New growth is slow to appear in spring. Usually sold as *A. goeringianum* 'Pictum'.

Ceratostigma plumbaginoides
(Plumbago larpentae)
Zone 6
Propagation: Division or cuttings

LEADWORT or PLUMBAGO

Deciduous to semi-evergreen
Exposure: Sun to light shade

This brightens any rock garden, border or underplanting with deep cobalt-blue flowers from August until frost. Leadwort, a rapidly spreading ground cover, has 8″-tall foliage which exhibits a beautiful copper color in autumn. Plants leaf out in spring later than most.

Chrysogonum virginianum
Zone 6
Propagation: Division or cuttings

GOLDENSTAR, GREEN-AND-GOLD
Evergreen or semi-deciduous
Exposure: Light shade to shade

This member of the Daisy Family is a moderately strong grower which prefers a well-drained soil in a partially shaded, sheltered position. It has star-like yellow blooms from spring to summer and grows to a height of 8″.

Andre Viette

Gary L. Koller

(Above left) In shady areas *Disporum sessile* 'Variegatum' covers quickly and produces bell-shaped, creamy-white spring flowers. (Above right) The shiny, dark green leaves of European ginger contrast well with the light green whorls of sweet woodruff. (Below) The blue-green foliage and lilac-blue flowers of dwarf crested iris lend interest to shady corners.

Andre Viette

Japanese painted fern *(Athyrium nipponicum* 'Pictum') comes in a wide choice of frond color and variegation, including silver, purple and cream.

Disporum sessile 'Variegatum' (No common name)
Zone 6 Deciduous
Propagation: Division Exposure: Shade

This woodland plant, which is derived from a species that is native to China and Japan, is related to fairy-bells. The beautiful lance-shaped leaves are cleanly striped with white, though slow to appear in spring. There are creamy white, bell-shaped flowers in spring. *Disporum sessile* 'Variegatum' grows to a height of 12″ to 14″ and will cover a shaded site quickly. A unique ground cover.

Epimedium alpinum ALPINE BARRENWORT
Zone 6 Deciduous to semi-evergreen
Propagation: Division
            Exposure: Light shade to shade (sun-tolerant if watered well in summer)

One of our finest ground covers, even surviving under trees where pachysandra and ivy have failed. This fast spreader grows to 8″ or 10″ in height and has great longevity. Its bright green foliage is touched with red and remains attractive for all but a few winter months. Light red-and-cream flowers in short sprays add charm to the garden before new leaves unfurl. *Epimedium pinnatum* (yellow flowers) also grows and multiplies well without attention. Both species tolerate dry shade.

Geranium sanguineum prostratum LANCASTER GERANIUM
(lancastriense)
Zone 3 Deciduous
Propagation: Division or cuttings Exposure: Sun or light shade

Lancaster geranium flourishes in a sandy, well-drained soil. It flowers most of the summer with light pink blooms veined in crimson. In addition to having value as a ground cover it is also a must for the rock garden.

Iris cristata DWARF CRESTED IRIS
Zone 3 Deciduous
Propagation: Division Exposure: Light shade to shade

This beautiful creeping iris enhances any shady spot with its lovely lilac-blue flowers and bluish-green foliage. Iris cristata is native to the eastern United States and grows to a height of 6″, with a moderate-to-fast spreading rate. Do not heavily mulch this iris as it will rot. A white form is also very showy.

Phlox stolonifera 'Blue Ridge'
Zone 2-3
Propagation: Division or cuttings

CREEPING BLUE PHLOX
Deciduous
Exposure: Light shade

This is a clear, light blue-flowered selection of a species which is native to Pennsylvania, Kentucky and Georgia. It grows moderately fast and graces the garden with beautiful flowers in April and May.

Potentilla tridentata minima
Zone 2
Propagation: Division or cuttings

DWARF THREE-TOOTHED CINQUEFOIL
Evergreen
Exposure: Sun

In spring this little cinquefoil exhibits white flowers above its foliage but they are not very showy. It is grown for its attractive, glossy, trifoliate leaves and the fact that it will tolerate dry rocky places. A rapid grower, the plant adds much interest to the ground-cover garden.

Rudbeckia fulgida 'Goldsturm'
Zone 5
Propagation: Division

PERENNIAL BLACK-EYED SUSAN
Deciduous
Exposure: Sun

This bright, showy plant provides three months of yellow summer color. It is a tall ground cover, growing to a height of 24". Perennial black-eyed Susan is a useful, durable plant to naturalize in a meadow.

Thymus serpyllum
Zone 3
Propagation: Division

CREEPING or WILD THYME
Evergreen
Exposure: Sun

Creeping thyme can be naturalized in the wild garden or used in a more formal ground-cover planting. Its purple flowers appear from late spring to summer, and the plant is valuable where a 2" mat is needed. Other prostrate thymes with white or red flowers are also excellent ground covers.

Uvularia grandiflora
Zone 3
Propagation: Division

BIG MERRYBELLS
Deciduous
Exposure: Light shade to shade

Merrybells' pendulous, 1"-long bell-shaped yellow flowers preceed attractive, bright green foliage in spring. This native American plant is extremely hardy and a very beautiful addition to the ground-cover garden. ❧

Andre Viette

In summer Lancaster geraniums bloom nearly continuously, producing crimson-veined light pink flowers.

New ideas for plant combinations . . .

MIXING BULBS AND PERENNIALS WITH GROUND COVERS

Michael H. Dodge

Covering the bare earth with a mass of plants that will tolerate poor growing conditions is a good garden practice, but it creates the problem of visual boredom if plantings are extensive. A large expanse of pachysandra or vinca is effective, but apart from flowers that disappear before one can notice them, it may lack interest after a time. A few durable perennials or bulbs artfully placed give seasonal appeal, while ferns can provide contrast in height and texture. Another approach is massing different kinds of ground covers.

There are two main types of ground covers, the low-growing or fine-leaved, and the taller or coarse-leaved plants. Of the wealth of plants available, select those that are hardy in your climate and which will receive the proper amount of light and moisture in your garden.

Soil preparation is necessary before planting. In dry, poor soils it is wise to mix in organic matter such as peat moss, manure or compost. Gypsum and coarse sand should be added to heavy, clay soils to improve drainage.

With Low-growing Ground Covers

Companion plants for such ground covers as ajuga or vinca should be small, or their leaves should go dormant in early summer to prevent smothering the ground cover. The dwarf windflowers (*Anemone* species), with their brightly-colored, daisy-shaped flowers, and their botanical relatives, the hepaticas (*H. americana, H. acutiloba*), are perfect. The lacy foliage and curiously-shaped, white flowers of Dutchman's breeches (*Dicentra cucullaria*) and its cousin, squirrel-corn

Although considered uncommon in the wild, Dutchman's breeches are one of the easiest woodland flowers to establish in the home garden.

(*D. canadensis*), are certain to attract interest.

Suitable dwarf bulbs include species crocus, which have daintier flowers than the better known Dutch hybrids. Winter aconite (*Eranthis hyemalis*), with yellow flowers, tinted green, is an attractive plant and is especially enhanced by spring snowflake (*Leucojum vernum*), whose white petals are tipped green or occasionally yellow. Miniature narcissus, such as *N. asturiensis* (*minimus* of the trade), *N.* 'Little Beauty' and *N.* 'Little Gem', are delightful and easily grown little daffodils. The species tulips, such as *T. pulchella* 'Violacea', *T. tarda* and *T. linifolia,* are charming and merit greater attention; dependably perennial, they have blossoms which last much longer than traditional hybrid tulips. Among the earliest other bulbs is *Scilla tubergeniana,* with porcelain-blue and white flowers that are able to withstand the rigors of late winter's cold and snowy weather.

The airy gracefulness of ferns reduces

Michael Dodge

Mixed ostrich fern, Solomon's seal and maidenhair fern give contrasting layers of color and texture.

For sparkle in the autumn add a few cyclamen (*C. neapolitanum, C. europaeum*) or fall crocus (*C. speciosus, C. zonatus*), but beware of the giant autumn-crocus (*Colchicum*) because its leaves will engulf large areas of low-growing ground covers.

When winter in the Northeast sends ajuga into dormancy and makes even periwinkle (*Vinca minor*) look rather sparse, a few evergreen wildflowers are welcome. Three attractive ones are Oconee-bells (*Shortia galacifolia*), galax (*G. urceolata;* formerly *aphylla*), and wild-ginger (*Asarum shuttleworthii* and *A. europaeum*). The first two also have exquisite spring blossoms, while the strange flowers of gingers are hidden beneath their leaves. The evergreen Christmas fern (*Polystichum acrostichoides*) shines throughout the winter, especially when partially covered with snow.

the monotony of some ground covers in summer. Maidenhair (*Adiantum pedatum*), and the hard-to-establish rattlesnake fern (*Botrychium virginianum*) are two handsome natives worth trying, as is the Japanese painted fern (*Athyrium nipponicum* 'Pictum') with its gray, green and burgundy-colored fronds. Summer-flowering perennials also help. A few suggestions: dwarf astilbes (*A. chinensis* 'Finale' and *A. c. pumila*), creeping lily-turf (*Liriope spicata*), and self-heal (*Prunella* 'Pink Loveliness' and 'White Loveliness').

With Taller-growing Ground Covers

Pachysandra, ivy and hosta can be interplanted with taller perennials and bulbs. The native merrybells (*Uvularia grandiflora*) with its yellow flowers cascading below bluish-green leaves deserves to be more widely grown. The starry flowers of bloodroot (*Sanguinaria canadensis*) and great white trillium (*T. grandiflorum*) put on a show before most ground covers recuperate from winter's onslaught. Two blue-flowered beauties, Virginia blue-bells (*Mertensia virginica*) and Siberian bugloss (*Brunnera macrophylla*), are easily grown; the latter has forget-me-not flowers and is usually sold as *Anchusa myosotidiflora*.

Some of the bulbs that can be naturalized under taller-growing ground covers are vigorous kinds of narcissus

The yellow flowers of the native merrybells can be a spring color punctuation to evergreen ground covers such as English ivy.

Michael Dodge

Few spring flowers rival the arresting beauty of the pure white bloodroot.

(trumpet, flat-cup and pheasant's-eye) and Spanish bluebells (*Endymion hispanicus;* formerly *Scilla campanulata*). The trout- and glacier-lilies (*Erythronium revolutum* and *E. grandiflorum*) are some of America's finest bulbs and will grow with hosta or ivy. The stars-of-Bethlehem are European bulbs with elegant white and jade-green petals, the nodding *Ornithogalum nutans* flowering in spring, and *O. pyramidale* in midsummer. For spring bloom, despite its name, plant the summer snowflake (*Leucojum aestivum*).

A few perennials that blossom in late spring and provide contrast in height should be considered. The white flowers of Solomon's-seal (*Polygonatum commutatum*), baneberries (*Actaea rubra* and *A. pachypoda*), and false Solomon's-seal (*Smilacina racemosa*) are not only attractive at this time of year, but they also have showy autumn fruit. For pure pleasure nothing is lovelier than the brightly colored flowers of columbine jauntily tossing their heads in the early summer breezes. Astilbes, with their white, pink or red plumes, can be used as a primary ground cover or interplanted with others, in sun or shade, provided adequate moisture is available. A few spikes of native fairy-candles (*Cimicifuga racemosa*) add interest in summer, and the related Kamtchatka fairy-candles (*C. simplex*) gives life to gardens in October when they have little else of which to boast. *Cimicifuga* is usually given the unflattering names of bugbane or snakeroot.

Ferns are ideal plants for growing with tall ground covers for differences in texture, which many people prefer to bloom. Christmas fern and spiny woodfern (*Dryopteris spinulosa*) are two handsome

George Taloumis

Blue fescue *(Festuca ovina glauca)* combines striking color with delicate texture in a perennial mounded grass.

Michael Dodge

Ozark phlox blends well with other flowers, particularly astilbe.

evergreens. Of the many deciduous kinds, try using marginal woodfern (*Dryopteris marginalis*), glade fern (*Athyrium pycnocarpon*), ostrich fern (*Matteuccia pensylvanica*), cinnamon fern (*Osmunda cinnamomea*) and its cousin the interrupted fern (*O. claytoniana*). These non-flowering plants are worthy of homage in early spring as their fiddleheads unfurl.

There are a few other perennial ground-cover combinations that have proven to be very successful. The rare Ozark phlox (*P. pilosa ozarkiana*) with its delicate pink flowers is most effective when planted amongst the bronze-leaved astilbes. At Winterthur, H. F. du Pont planted a bed of the late-summer-flowering blue leadwort (*Ceratòstigma plumbaginoides*) with the brilliant yellow of the so-called fall-daffodil (*Sternbergia lutea*). Although *Sternbergia* is related to narcissus, it looks more like a crocus. It has shiny, dark green leaves which are produced at blossom-time, and go dormant in spring. These colors, yellow and blue, can be repeated in spring with a dwarf forsythia, *F. viridissima* 'Bronxensis', and *Scilla sibirica* 'Spring Beauty'. Another early spring display of white epimedium (*E. youngianum* 'Niveum') with white grape-hyacinth (*Muscari botryoides* 'Album') brightens up a corner of the garden and requires little attention. The taller Armenian grape-hyacinth (*Muscari armeniacum*) will give early color to a planting of the lily-turf named after it (*Liriope muscari*). (The similarity between the flowers of these, appearing in different seasons, reminds us how often nature mimics herself.) For dry, sunny spots the stonecrops (*Sedum*), hens-and-chicks (*Sempervivum*) and prickly-pear cactus (*Opuntia humifusa*) utilize otherwise wasted ground.

A technique inspired by the Brazilian landscape designer, Roberto Burle Marx, is to use mass plantings of three or four ground covers with different foliage colors or textures, in curvilinear beds that echo the surrounding landscape. Following are some of the perennials that can be used in this manner.

PLANTS WITH GRAY FOLIAGE: Lamb's ears (*Stachys byzantina;* formerly *lanata*), pearly-everlasting (*Anaphalis margaritacea*), pussy-toes (*Antennaria dioica* 'Rosea'), pinks (*Dianthus*), blue fescue (*Festuca ovina glauca*), rue (*Ruta graveolens* 'Blue Beauty'), Silver Mound artemisia (*A. schmidtiana* 'Nana') and blue-leaved plantain-lily (*Hosta sieboldiana*).

PLANTS WITH YELLOW FOLIAGE: Golden money wort (*Lysimachia nummularia* 'Aurea'), golden thyme (*Thymus vulgaris* 'Aureus'), golden feverfew (*Chrysanthemum parthenium* 'Aureum') and golden meadowsweet (*Filipendula ulmaria* 'Aurea').

PLANTS WITH VARIEGATED FOLIAGE: Tricolor sage (*Salvia officinalis* 'Tricolor'), goutweed (*Aegopodium podagraria* 'Variegatum'), silver-edge pachysandra (*P. terminalis* 'Variegata'), dead-nettles (*Lamium maculatum* cultivars), and variegated forms of some grasses (*Molinia caerulea, Carex morrowi, Miscanthus sinensis* and the beautiful *Hakonechloa macra*).

PLANTS WITH RED OR BRONZE FOLIAGE: Bronze-leaf ajuga (*A. reptans* 'Gaiety' or *A. r.* 'Bronze Beauty'), purpled-leaved sage (*Salvia officinalis* 'Purpurea'), dwarf lily-turf (*Ophiopogon planiscapus* 'Nigrescens'), bronze-leaf stonecrop (*Sedum maximum* 'Atropurpureum'), firecracker sundrop (*Oenothera tetragona* 'Illumination'), and bronze-leaf Rodgersia (*R. podophylla*). ❧

27

There are rugged and dependable . . .

GROUND COVERS FOR THE FAR NORTH

Roger Vick

The University of Alberta Devonian Botanic Garden was founded in 1959. For some 20 years the Garden has introduced and tested a wide variety of ornamental plants and evaluated their potential for central Alberta.

Severe temperatures and desiccation both take their toll, restricting the number of satisfactory trees and shrubs that can be grown in this region. On the other hand, a wide selection of herbaceous perennials are grown in central Alberta and throughout the Canadian prairies, protected by a more-or-less reliable snow cover for much of the six-month winter. This discussion of ground covers includes only those species that are reliably hardy not only here but also in areas of even lower precipitation and unreliable winter snow cover.

Climate

The yearly mean temperature is 37°F (3°C), with a peak minimum of −56°F (−49°C), and peak maximum of 98°F (37°C). The last spring frost date falls on about June 1st and the first autumn frost occurs about September 4th (all dates are mean statistics). This allows a frost-free growing season of some 95 days. The start of the growing season for perennials—mean temperature above 42°F (5.5°C)—is April 23rd, and the end of the season is October 8th.

Precipitation is not high. The annual mean is 19 in. (47 cm.), with 5.1 in. or 13 cm. equivalent being snow. The average humidity is 61%. A midsummer day-length of 17 hours allows plants to make the most of a short season.

Ground Covers

With the exception of *Juniperus horizontalis,* a low evergreen, and *Eriogonum umbellatum,* which is sub-shrubby, the following ground covers are herbaceous perennials. All are readily propagated by division, although *Dianthus deltoides* is best increased from seed. Most of the following ground covers retain foliage through winter, but this is of little consequence where they are blanketed by snow until spring.

Aegopodium podagraria 'Variegatum' (Goutweed). Only the variegated form, with white-margined foliage, is normally offered commercially. It tolerates shade and is one of our most vigorous and reliable ground covers.

Because it can become invasive, goutweed is best used where there is a physical barrier between it and lawns or other plantings such as between the side of a building and a path where the roots will be contained. It produces an attractive effect in island beds and is used in parking-lot dividers.

Cerastium tomentosum (Snow-in-summer) is sometimes scorned as being too easy to grow, but this is a definite advantage in ground cover situations. The low spreading mounds of silvery foliage are ornamental in themselves but are further enhanced by twinkling white stars of flowers in spring and early summer. If left undisturbed for a number of years the center tends to die out, so it is best to lift the roots and divide them with a sharp spade every second or third season just prior to spring growth. Plants spaced up to three feet apart will fill in within two or three months. Very happy in sun and well drained soils.

Dianthus deltoides (Maiden Pink) can be relied upon to form dense low mats and to spread vegetatively and by seed. The foliage is of fine, dark green texture, and the red, white or pink flowers appear profusely in spring and early summer. Cultivars such as 'Brilliancy' are available. Propagation is by seed, which is best sown *in situ* in late autumn, to germinate the following spring.

Aegopodium podagraria variegatum, or variegated goutweed, is a handsome ground cover, despite its rather pedestrian name. A physical barrier is needed between it and lawns because the roots can be invasive.

Eriogonum umbellatum (Umbrella-plant) is rarely seen in gardens but is native to the Alberta foothills and has been used to good purpose in sunny locations. In milder regions *Eriogonum* species suffer from winter wet but on the Canadian prairies have proven perfectly hardy and densely mat-forming. The flowers, borne in umbels on stems about 8 in. (20 cm.) tall, are pale yellow becoming tinged with rose as they age. Foliage produces autumn tints. Although it spreads steadily, the umbrella-plant is not invasive. Propagation by division.

Fragaria virginiana (Wild Strawberry) has the advantage of being hardy, and it is easily propagated from self-rooting stolons. The more adventurous gardener may wish to accept a little more height and try one of the fine fruiting cultivars.

Glechoma hederacea 'Variegata' (Variegated Creeping Charlie) has obtained a bad name where allowed to colonize lawns, alpine gardens or other choice plantings. However, in sunny or shady areas where root barriers can be used this green-and-yellow foliage plant can be relied upon to succeed as a ground cover.

Juniperus horizontalis. Creeping juniper is often overlooked as a ground cover, possibly because of the initial expense. Certain cultivars such as 'Prince of Wales' and 'Douglasii' are excellent for sunny, well-drained locations. Their main disadvantage is that, in order to obtain a satisfactory effect in the first two or three years, they should be planted about one foot apart. In later years they spread to nine feet or more in diameter, necessitating the removal of alternate plants.

Lysimachia nummularia (Creeping Jenny, Moneywort) is a small-leaved, prostrate grower valued for its success in moist and shady areas. In such locations it will spread very rapidly by creeping stems. Flowers are bright yellow in midsummer. There is also a golden-leaved cultivar. Propagation is by division.

Potentilla anserina sericea (Silverweed) prefers moist and sunny locations but will

29

Dianthus, dwarf *Euonymus alata*, lilies and rosemary line the terrace while thyme is used as an exceptionally fragrant ground cover.

tolerate adversity with little complaint. The silvery foliage is pinnately divided, providing a fine texture. The plant creeps with confidence by stolons in the manner of the strawberry. The yellow flowers take second place to the foliage. As with many successful ground covers, silverweed should not be planted in close proximity to less robust species.

Thymus serpyllum (Wild Thyme, Mother-of-thyme) and closely related species. Densely mat-forming, low and very suitable for sunny, well-drained places. The deep pink flowers are borne profusely, often smothering the center of the plant to death, leaving only the vegetative growth around the outside to continue the following season. Wild thyme, which is readily divided, is popular as a soil binder in light soils that are subject to erosion. Volunteer seedlings may become weedy in choice plantings. ❧

GROUND COVERS FOR SOUTHWESTERN GARDENS

Carl Zangger

The Southwest is a unique region of the United States in that the climate can be so variable. It ranges from subtropical in the coastal areas of southern California to alpine in the mountains to extremely dry in the desert areas. In fact, within the range of just a few miles it is possible to experience all these conditions. However, much of the Southwest is arid, experiencing little or no rainfall for several months of the year. Supplemental irrigation or watering systems are a must for successful gardens.

It is difficult to generalize in recommending plant varieties for such a varied region. Gardeners are urged to determine the climate in which they plan to plant before actually making a selection. Local arboretums, university cooperative extension services, as well as landscape architects, contractors and nurserymen are all sources of help both for determining the climate and securing information on plant varieties.

The following list is not intended to be complete, but it comprises the varieties most frequently used in this region.

Ajuga BUGLE Zone 4 Sun or Shade
Very popular in most of the Southwest. The majority are rapid growers and form a thick carpet of attractive green or bronze foliage through the growing season. In milder parts of our area they are nearly evergreen. Flowers, usually blue, are profuse in spring, nearly hiding the foliage. Ajugas benefit from reasonably well-drained soil and require plenty of moisture. They may be grown in full sun in most areas provided they receive adequate watering, but shade is preferable in the hot inland valleys. There are several widely planted kinds: low-growing *A. reptans*, *A. r.* 'Atropurpurea', and taller variants including crisp-leaved 'Jungle Green' and 'Jungle Bronze'.

Arctotheca calendula CAPE WEED
Zone 9 Sun
There is hardly a day of the year when this attractive low-grower is not displaying its single yellow daisy-like flowers in profusion. It grows rapidly, forming a thick bed of gray-green foliage that is retained in winter. Cape weed spreads rapidly by runners and is excellent for erosion control on banks. Good in borders, too. Tolerant of heat and drought. Grows best in improved soil, but appearance acceptable in relatively poor soil.

Los Angeles Times

Ornamental strawberry *(Fragaria chiloensis)* fills in quickly with runners and can be mowed to freshen the appearance.

Baccharis pilularis COYOTE-BUSH
Zone 8 Sun
This California native is a real problem solver. It is drought tolerant yet performs well in high-rainfall areas if drainage is fast. Fairly rapid growth, to 2' in height, and spreading to 3-4'. Candidate for a steep bank, where it will naturally drape to the contour of the land. Evergreen, attractive year-round. Flowers rather inconspicuous; sexes are borne on different plants. Nurseries usually propagate the male form because the female sets cottony seed heads which can be a nuisance when they ripen and blow about.

Campanula poscharskyana
SERBIAN BELLFLOWER Zone 3 Shade
In spring this hardy variety puts on a display of small lavender-blue flowers that nearly hide the foliage. Leaves are round, ½-¾" in diameter. Plants grow normally 6-10" in height and spread from underground roots, forming a solid bed when mature. Serbian bellflower is an excellent filler under shrubs and one of the relatively few plants that will perform well in shade. Provide reasonably good soil and plenty of water. *Campanula garganica,* Dalmatian bellflower, is similar but slightly smaller, both in growth and in flower. Flowers are violet-blue and star-shaped.

Cerastium tomentosum SNOW-IN-SUMMER
Zone 2 Sun
Attractive little creeper with silver foliage. In spring it is a snowbank of small white starry flowers. The rest of the year *Cerastium* presents a relatively neat gray-green carpet about 6" high. If growth becomes uneven, it may be trimmed back lightly. Drought tolerant and requiring little care. Not fussy about soil but should have reasonably good drainage.

Fragaria chiloensis ORNAMENTAL STRAWBERRY Zone 8 Sun or light shade
Dark green leaves form a thick cover 6-8" high. Attractive single, white, yellow-centered flowers in spring. Sends out runners which root as they grow. Give regular and ample watering. Plants may be mowed once a year to eliminate old growth and provide fresher appearance. A parent of the garden strawberry.

Gazania SOUTH AFRICAN DAISY
Zone 9 Sun
In southern California particularly, this plant is one of the most colorful and longest flowering of any ground cover. There is hardly a season when gazanias are not in bloom with their 2"-wide flowers of brilliant colors, mostly in shades of yellow, orange, bronze, white and combi-

A splendid warm-climate perennial, gazania can also be used as an annual in the North.

nations. They are drought resistant, grow rapidly and perform well in relatively poor soil. Generally available in two principal growth types—clumping and trailing. CLUMPING TYPES include: 'Copper King'—huge 4-5", bronze red; 'Fiesta Red'—copper red, dark foliage; 'Gold Rush'—clear golden orange, black-ringed center. TRAILING GAZANIA is available in yellow, orange, bronze and white. Plants have clean silver-gray foliage, grow 6-10" tall, make a rapid cover and look good all year. Excellent for both banks and beds.

Algerian and English Ivies
Zone 5-9   Sun or shade
One of our most widely used plant groups because of clean, fresh, year-round appearance and ease of culture. Ivies appreciate ample summer watering. There are many types to choose from. The following are among the best and most widely used:

Hedera canariensis ALGERIAN IVY Zone 7, 8. Big dark green leaves, often 6" across; for banks and borders.

Algerian ivy *(Hedera canariensis)*

Hedera helix ENGLISH IVY Zone 5. Hardy, grows and spreads rapidly, provides dense cover; dark green, heavily veined leaves 2-3" across. *H. h.* 'Hahn's Self-branching' ('Hahnii') Zone 6. Smaller, lighter green leaves than typical English ivy and slightly less vigorous; more compact and softer effect. *H. h.* 'Needlepoint' Zone 6—a much smaller leaf than 'Hahn's Self-branching,' and with sharp-pointed tip; good dark green color and compact growth habit.

Iceplant   Various species
Zones 8-10   Sun
Several kinds, all succulents, with varying growth habits. In California this group is one of the most widely used for ground covers. Of rapid growth and drought tolerant; most are spectacular in bloom. The following are often seen:

Carpobrotus edulis FIG-MARIGOLD Zone 9. Rugged, heavy, three-cornered leaves 3-4" long. Big 3"-wide cream-colored flower. Height: 10-12".

Delosperma 'Alba' WHITE ICEPLANT Zone 9. One-inch triangular leaves and olive-green color. Small white flowers. Height 6-8".

English ivy *(Hedera helix)*

Drosanthemum hispidum ROSEA ICE-PLANT Zone 10. A blanket of lavender pink in spring. Low mat-like growth, 4-6″ high. One of the best for steep slopes.

Lampranthus aurantiacus BUSH-TYPE ICE-PLANT Zone 9. Blooms early spring; yellow, gold and orange flowers. Low bushy growth 10-15″ tall. Excellent for borders and beds.

Lampranthus productus PURPLE ICE-PLANT Zone 9. Earliest to bloom, starting in January and continuing for months. Bright purple color is spectacular. Spreading growth habit. 10 to 12″ tall.

Lampranthus spectabilis TRAILING ICE-PLANT Zone 9. Blooms are red, rose, light pink, lavender and purple. A blanket of fluorescent color. Trailing growth habit. Gray-green foliage 6-12″ tall.

Maleophora (Hymenocyclus) crocea purpureocrocea CROCEUM ICEPLANT Zone 8. Most frost-hardy of iceplants and one of the toughest. One-to-two-inch gray-green leaves. Coppery-red or yellow flowers most of the year.

Lonicera japonica 'Halliana' HALL'S JAPANESE HONEYSUCKLE Zone 5 Sun
One of our hardiest woody vines and used successfully over most of North America, though a familiar escape in the South. In California it is planted extensively on banks from the seashore to the mountains and deserts. Height as a ground cover: 2′. Plants spread rapidly and grow well in almost any soil. Light green foliage is retained year-round where winters are mild, but plants go dormant in areas with cold winter temperatures. A generous bloomer in summer with attractive yellow flowers that are pleasantly fragrant. There is also a bronze-leaved variety.

Ophiopogon japonicus MONDO-GRASS Zone 6 Sun or shade.
Dark grass-like foliage is evergreen. Plants form clumps about 10″ tall and eventually become very dense. Extremely adaptable and can be planted in sun in all but desert areas. Does equally well in shade. Appreciates ample amounts of water in summer particularly if grown in sun. Mondo-grass requires little attention and may be used as borders or mass plantings, where it will look the same at every season.

Osteospermum fruticosum TRAILING AFRICAN DAISY Zone 9 Sun
Few plants can equal this daisy for a dazzling display of spring and summer bloom. Big (2″-wide) flowers, ranging from white to purple in color, hide foliage during bloom period. Rapid growing, reaching a height of 18″ and sending out runners 2-3′ long. Foliage is bright green all year. Drought resistant but requires summer watering. Excellent for planting on hillsides, also along roadway banks. For this reason plants are often referred to as Freeway Daisies. Osteospermum is planted from the seashore to the inland valleys and even the warmer desert areas. Because this daisy grows vigorously it is sometimes necessary to prune in autumn to remove some of the accumulated old growth.

Phyla nodiflora (Lippia canescens repens) LIPPIA Zone 9 Sun
A good lawn substitute, lippia sends out strong runners that form a tightly knit sod. It may be mowed or left to grow naturally. Height: 6″. In summer it blooms with little button-like, lavender-pink flowers of which bees are fond. Thrives in heat. Semi-dormant in winter but never entirely brown. Tolerates considerable traffic and is often used in parking strips for that reason. Though drought resistant, lippia must have a fair amount of summer watering to look its brightest.

Potentilla verna SPRING CINQUEFOIL Zone 6 Sun or light shade
This plant with strawberry-like leaves is one of the most trouble-free available. Runners spread rapidly and are clothed in dark green foliage that is evergreen in mild areas. Forms a thick, tough mat 3-6″ high. In spring and early summer it blooms heavily with charming ½″-wide, buttercup-like flowers of bright yellow. If it becomes untidy, it may be mowed and will quickly regrow. Useful in any size spaces, on banks or flat areas, in sun or shade. In our region spring cinquefoil appreciates watering and will look its brightest if fertilized from time to time.

Rosmarinus officinalis **'Prostratus'** PROS-
TRATE ROSEMARY   Zone 8   Sun
The dark evergreen foliage of this spreading shrub is attractive the year around. It
will grow 2½' tall and spread 4' or more.
In spring and summer abundant light blue
flowers are produced. Rosemary is not
particular about soil and seems to adapt
well wherever used. Planted on banks it
will follow the contour of the slope and
even drape over a wall. Drought and wind
resistant.

Saxifraga stolonifera (sarmentosa)
STRAWBERRY-BEGONIA   Zone 7   Shade
Ground covers for shade are not plentiful
here, but in frost-free areas this does an
excellent job. Height: generally not over
6". The rounded leaves with red veins are
2" wide, attractive all year. Spring
bonus—tall spikes of dainty white to soft
pink flowers. Plants must have a fairly
moist condition to grow well. They also
benefit from a humus-rich soil.

Sedum   STONECROP   Zone 3-8   Sun
There are many types in this group of
succulents. Some reach several feet in
height, others are low creepers. The
majority are not particular about soils and
will be found persisting even in very poor
rocky areas but, like most plants, perform
better under good garden conditions. For
the most part drought resistant, in the
Southwest they should receive modest
amounts of water through the dry seasons. Following are a few of the low
creepers that are outstanding for ground
covers: *Sedum anglicum*—2-3" high, yellow flowers in spring; *S. brevifolium*—2-
3" high, white flowers; *S.* x *rubrotinctum*
(*guatemalense*)—6-8" tall, bronzy red
foliage, yellow flowers; *S. spurium*
'Dragon's Blood'—3-4" high, bronzy
rosette foliage, rosy red bloom.

Soleirola (Helxine) soleirolii   BABY TEARS,
HELXINE   Zone 9   Shade
For shady, relatively frost-free areas this
delightful little carpeter is one of the few
plants that really performs well. It needs
plenty of moisture and grows moderately
fast, covering the ground with a bright
green carpet of tiny round leaves that
look the same at every season. Nice
under other shade-loving plants but can
be used around stepping stones, in rock
gardens, bonsai dishes and terrariums. It

Croceum iceplant in bloom

Los Angeles Times

M. Joyner

Several varieties of stonecrop *(Sedum)* planted vertically in a stone wall.

is undemanding as to soil. Growth is generally under 6″ and may be trimmed so plants cling tightly to the ground.

Vinca major BIG PERIWINKLE Zone 7 Sun or shade

A very rugged plant for covering banks and steep slopes. May be planted from the seashore to the mountains. In desert areas shade is required. Dark green oval leaves on trailing stems root as they spread. Excellent for erosion control. It grows rapidly, 18-24″ tall, in nearly all soils. In spring there is a wealth of 1″-wide blue flowers. Aging plantings may be mowed in winter to remove old thatch and give a more uniform spring and summer appearance. Appreciates and looks best with plenty of water but will tolerate some dryness.

Vinca minor PERIWINKLE, MYRTLE Zone 4 Sun or shade

Foliage is smaller and darker than *V. major.* It also grows less vigorously and lower (12″). Makes a dense cover with nice year-round appearance. In spring it blooms heavily with attractive blue flowers about ¾″ in diameter. Should receive plenty of water in the hotter months. ✿

Baby's tears or helxine, a dense ground cover with very tiny leaves.

Hank Hoag

VINES IN CALIFORNIA
Philip E. Chandler

Drier and more variable climatically than south Florida and the far south of Texas, California in its mildest portions grows most of the vines recommended for both temperate and humid subtropical zones. Notable tender evergreen climbers common in southern California include:

EASTER-LILY VINE (*Beaumontia grandiflora*). Very large-leaved, woody-stemmed twiner best grown on strong arbor; fragrant white chalice-like flowers in generous clusters spring through warm season. Place in lee of prevailing wind where warmth accumulates.

BOUGAINVILLEA hybrids grown for brilliant flower bracts. Plant in hottest location; strong reflected light is beneficial, also occasional deep watering once established. Magenta and most red-flowered forms rampant; burnt-orange to salmon and gold cultivars less vigorous; pinks and near-white weak growers. Foliage poor in cold weather.

KANGAROO VINE (*Cissus antarctica*), with leathery, simple leaves, is rampant in sun or shade, in dry or wet soil. Effective for ground cover or screening, particularly for covering chain-link fence. Quiet, neutral green, tenacious.
    C. hypoglauca, perhaps the most decorative of the *Cissus,* has palmately compound leaves with coppery new growth, conspicuous tendrils. *C. rhombifolia*— leaves more openly structured than above; useful as ground cover, climber or spiller; shear for density. *Rhoicissus capensis* suggests an evergreen form of the domestic grape; very bronzy new growth and tendrils, bright surfaced, rather large, simple leaves, some deeply lobed.

ORCHID TRUMPET VINE (*Clytostoma callistegioides; Bignonia violacea*). Pinkish-lavender trumpet flowers are conspicuous in late spring. Plants take sun or considerable shade, almost any soil. Few predators or diseases.

RED TRUMPET VINE (*Distictis buccinatoria*) is a rampant grower with magnificent dark foliage. Hanging clusters of large yellow-throated orange-red flowers fade rose-red, from midspring to winter; sun, filtered shade. *D. laxiflora,* the vanilla-scented trumpet vine, is a slow grower with foliage not so dense or glossy. Light blue-purple flowers fade

Bougainvillea, the ubiquitous warm climate vine, thrives on heat and strong light.

J. Horace McFarland

pale lavender, summer through autumn. *D.* 'Rivers' is like the red trumpet vine except flowers are rosy purple with near-orange throat; foliage is less abundant, growth slower.

CAROLINA JESSAMINE (*Gelsemium sempervirens*), described elsewhere in this Handbook for other zones, is almost fool-proof in sun or light shade. It flowers from late autumn through spring and is not rampant in California.

Hardenbergia comptoniana is a vigorous, open-textured vine for sun or light shade. Small purple pea-shaped flowers in drooping clusters are conspicuous from late January to April; narrow trifoliate leaves subject to leafeaters.

WAX VINE (*Hoya carnosa*), a dull-green climbing succulent, can cope with full shade, even dry shade, and poor air circulation. Tolerates containers, limited root room. Summer flowers are dusty pink, waxen.

Mandevilla 'Alice du Pont' is a tender twiner for a very protected exposure. Flowers are large, funnel-form, clustered, strongly pink, continuous with warm weather. Handsome ribbed leaves become sparse in winter.

Pandorea (*Tecoma*) *jasminoides.* Light green, pinnate leaves form open structure. Conspicuous flowers are pinkish white with crimson throat, abundant in summer, autumn. Variety *rosea* is lavender-pink and *alba* pure white. All appreciate accumulated heat, protection from ocean wind.

Stephanotis floribunda. This elegant dark green, oval-leaved twiner can be effectively trained on heavy chain from eaves. Large-clustered flowers, borne in summer, are white, waxen, fragrant. Plant where roots are shaded, vine in half-day sun.

CAPE-HONEYSUCKLE (*Tecomaria capensis*) is an extremely vigorous climbing (or spilling) shrub. Leaves are handsomely pinnate, deep green; flowers are red-orange in upright terminal clusters, especially conspicuous late summer into winter. Plants take hottest sun or partial shade. No pests. ❧

Ground Covers for Semi-Arid Regions

This area comprises southern Nevada, southern Utah, California desert regions, Arizona, New Mexico and southwestern Texas. It is very diverse in climate, but one common feature is low rainfall combined with high summer heat. Some parts such as the low deserts of southern California and Arizona experience minimal winter frosts; the higher plateaus are subject to severely cold winter temperatures. Soils generally need the addition of humus, and a supplementary watering system is essential. Spring and autumn applications of high-nitrogen fertilizer are usually desirable. Soil pH tends to be high and water quality is variable, often saline. As in other areas, the gardener is urged to consult with local extension authorities and other horticultural sources concerning appropriate ground covers.

Many of the ground covers on the previous list are used here—cape weed, trailing gazania, coyote bush, lippia, Hall's Japanese honeysuckle, spring cinquefoil, prostrate rosemary and big periwinkle. Other ground covers of note: Sprengeri-fern (*Asparagus densiflorus* 'Sprengeri') (Zone 9) (sun or shade), whose soft plumy foliage reaches a height of 18″ and creates a billowy effect; gray lavender-cotton (*Santolina chamaecyparissus*) (Zone 6) (sun), with soft yellow button-like flowers in summer and height of 18-24″ which may be kept lower by trimming; prostrate germander (*Teucrium chamaedrys* 'Prostratum') (Zone 5) (sun), having small, bright green leaves retained nearly year round in milder areas, 4-6″ spikes of rosy-lavender blooms, and a height of 8-10″. It is deeply rooted and binds the soil well.

—Carl Zangger ❧

Summer grape *(Vitis aestivalis)*

VINES FOR EVERY PURPOSE

Whether for showy flowers, colorful fruits, fine foliage or special situations, selection is all important

Donald Wyman

Vines should be selected with great care. It will be most helpful to go through catalogs or to visit nurserymen or botanic gardens because too often the popular one is not the best. To help select the right type, the fol-lowing will be useful. Not a list of "the best" vines, (almost every one of them has its limitations), nevertheless it should aid in the search for just the right vine for a par-ticular purpose.

Henry clematis *(C. lawsoniana* 'Henryi')

For Flowers

There are many of these, both slow and fast growing. Some, like the wisterias, fail to flower satisfactorily under certain conditions; and others, like the clematis clan, require special care and soil in order to produce a profusion of flowers. On the other hand, the fleece vine and the trumpet creeper will grow well under many different conditions, and so, naturally, are among those that are frequently seen. Some of the others are decidedly worth trying in order to produce good flowers, and a close study of the articles in this Handbook will aid materially in this respect. Flowering periods vary from place to place. The dates given here are for northeastern United States except the ones for vines that grow only in warm climates, marked (W). Hardiness zones are taken from the Hardiness Map of the Arnold Arboretum (inside back cover).

Common Name	Scientific Name	Time of Blooming	Hardiness Zone
BLOOM MORE OR LESS CONTINUOUSLY IN WARM CLIMATES			
Coralvine	*Antigonon leptopus*	Continuously	9
Glorybower	*Clerodendrum speciosum*	Continuously	9
Bleedingheart glorybower	*Clerodendrum thomsoniae*	Continuously	9
Mexican blood trumpet vine	*Distictis buccinatoria*	May-Sept. or all year in some places	10
Maypop, Passion flower	*Passiflora incarnata*	Continuously	7
Jasmine nightshade	*Solanum jasminoides*	Continuously	9
SPRING AND EARLY SUMMER BLOOM			
Anemone clematis	*Clematis montana*	May-June	6
Pink clematis	*Clematis montana rubens*	May-June	5
Yellow honeysuckle	*Lonicera flava*	May-June	5
Cherokee rose	*Rosa laevigata*	May	7
Rambler rose		June	4-5
Chinese star-jasmine	*Trachelospermum jasminoides*	April-July	7-8
Japanese wisteria	*Wisteria floribunda*	May	4
Long-cluster Japanese wisteria	*Wisteria floribunda* 'Macrobotrys'	May	4
Pink Japanese wisteria	*Wisteria floribunda* 'Rosea'	May	4
Chinese wisteria	*Wisteria sinensis*	May	5

Common Name	Scientific Name	Time of Blooming	Hardiness Zone
SUMMER BLOOM			
Trumpet creeper	*Campsis radicans*	mid-July-Sept.	4
Curly clematis	*Clematis crispa*	June-Aug.	5
Stanavoi clematis	*Clematis fusca*	June-Aug.	5
Jackman clematis	*Clematis jackmanii*	mid-July	5
Henry clematis	*Clematis lawsoniana henryi*	June-Aug.	5
Italian clematis	*Clematis viticella*	June-Aug.	5
Kermes clematis	*Clematis viticella kermesina*	June-Aug.	5
Climbing hydrangea	*Hydrangea anomala petiolaris*	June-July	4
Everblooming honeysuckle	*Lonicera heckrottii*	June-Sept.	5
honeysuckle	*Lonicera henryi*	June-Aug.	4
Hall's Japanese honeysuckle	*Lonicera japonica* 'Halliana'	June-Sept.	4
Woodbine honeysuckle	*Lonicera periclymenum*	June-Aug'.	4
Trumpet honeysuckle	*Lonicera sempervirens*	May-Aug.	3
Tellmann honeysuckle	*Lonicera tellmanniana*	June-Sept.	5
Chinese honeysuckle	*Lonicera tragophylla*	June	6
Passion flower	*Passiflora caerulea*	June-Sept. (W)	7-8
Bengal clockvine	*Thunbergia grandiflora*	midsummer (W)	8
Regel's threewingnut	*Tripterygium regelii*	July	4
LATE SUMMER AND FALL BLOOM			
October clematis	*Clematis apiifolia*	Sept.-Oct.	4
Jouin clematis	*Clematis jouiniana*	Aug.-Oct.	4
Western virgin's bower	*Clematis ligusticifolia*	Aug.-Sept.	5
Sweet autumn clematis	*Clematis paniculata*	Sept.-Oct.	5
Scarlet clematis	*Clematis texensis*	July-Sept.	5
Virgin's bower	*Clematis virginiana*	Aug.-Sept.	5
Cup-and-saucer vine	*Cobaea scandens*	July-frost	9
Tanglehead	*Pileostegia viburnoides*	late Aug.-Sept. (W)	7
Silver fleece-vine	*Polygonum aubertii*	Aug.-Sept.	4
Memorial rose	*Rosa wichuraiana*	Aug.-Sept.	5
Costa Rican nightshade	*Solanum wendlandii*	July-Oct. (W)	9

Scarlet clematis
(C. texensis) in flower

Virgin's bower *(Clematis virginiana)* seed pods

For Colorful Fruits

Common Name	Scientific Name	Time of Blooming	Hardiness Zone
Porcelain ampelopsis	*Ampelopsis brevipedunculata*	autumn	4
Oriental bittersweet	*Celastrus orbiculata*	autumn-winter	4
American bittersweet	*Celastrus scandens*	autumn-winter	2
Clematis	*Clematis*-most species	summer-autumn	4-5
Big-leaf wintercreeper or evergreen bittersweet	*Euonymus fortunei vegeta*	autumn	5
Running euonymus	*Euonymus obovata*	autumn	3
Scarlet kadsura	*Kadsura japonica*	autumn	7
	Parthenocissus species	autumn	3-4
Himalayan magnolia-vine	*Schisandra propinqua*	autumn	8

Open Growing

The following vines should not be selected for a screen. They do not make a dense mass of foliage, but they do have merit in adding the beauty of foliage outline to the interesting architectural features of a trellis or lattice work.

Common Name	Scientific Name	Hardiness Zone
Porcelain ampelopsis	*Ampelopsis brevipedunculata*	4
Curly clematis	*Clematis crispa*	5
Jackman clematis	*Clematis jackmanii*	5
Jouin clematis	*Clematis jouiniana*	4
Western virgin's bower	*Clematis ligusticifolia*	5
Golden clematis	*Clematis tangutica obtusiuscula*	5
Kermes clematis	*Clematis viticella* 'Kermesina'	5
Everblooming honeysuckle	*Lonicera heckrottii*	5
Woodbine honeysuckle	*Lonicera periclymenum*	4
Trumpet honeysuckle	*Lonicera sempervirens*	3
Tellmann honeysuckle	*Lonicera tellmanniana*	5
Chinese honeysuckle	*Lonicera tragophylla*	6
Firecracker vine	*Manettia glabra*	10
Virginia creeper	*Parthenocissus quinquefolia*	3
Cherokee rose	*Rosa laevigata*	7

Rapidly Growing

If one wishes a vine rather than a shrub or a tree to cover some unsightly obstacle quickly or to provide a screen in a short time, these are the vines for this purpose. They are all fairly dense in habit and any one of them can be made denser merely by a little pruning. In this group will be found clinging vines as well as those that twine.

Common Name	Scientific Name	Hardiness Zone
Bower actinidia	*Actinidia arguta*	4
Chinese gooseberry	*Actinidia chinensis*	7
Kolomikta actinidia	*Actinidia kolomikta*	4
Silvervine actinidia	*Actinidia polygama*	4
Fiveleaf akebia	*Akebia quinata*	4
Pepper-vine	*Ampelopsis arborea*	7
Porcelain ampelopsis	*Ampelopsis brevipedunculata*	4
Coralvine	*Antigonon leptopus*	9
Dutchman's pipe	*Aristolochia durior*	4
Crossvine	*Bignonia capreolata*	6
Trumpet creeper	*Campsis radicans*	4
Oriental bittersweet	*Celastrus orbiculata*	4
American bittersweet	*Celastrus scandens*	2
Anemone clematis	*Clematis montana*	6
Sweet autumn clematis	*Clematis paniculata*	5
Scarlet clematis	*Clematis texensis*	5
Virgin's bower	*Clematis virginiana*	4
Travelers' joy	*Clematis vitalba*	4
Italian clematis	*Clematis viticella*	5
Cup-and-saucer vine	*Cobaea scandens*	9
Mexican blood trumpet vine	*Distictis buccinatoria*	10
Creeping fig	*Ficus pumila*	9
English ivy	*Hedera helix*	5
Hall's Japanese honeysuckle	*Lonicera japonica* 'Halliana'	4
Trumpet honeysuckle	*Lonicera sempervirens*	3
Catclaw vine	*Macfadyena unguis-cati*	8
Moonseed	*Menispermum canadense*	5
Wirevine	*Muehlenbeckia complexa*	6
Virginia creeper	*Parthenocissus quinquefolia*	3
Japanese creeper (Boston Ivy)	*Parthenocissus tricuspidata*	4
Passion flowers	*Passiflora* species	7-8
Silver fleece vine	*Polygonum aubertii*	4
Chinese star-jasmine	*Trachelospermum jasminoides*	7-8
Glory vine grape	*Vitis coignetiae*	5
Japanese wisteria	*Wisteria floribunda*	4
Chinese wisteria	*Wisteria sinensis*	5

Kudzu (*Pueraria lobata*), from Japan, was widely planted in the South in the early part of the 20th century, mainly for soil conservation and as a food source for cattle. It was also sometimes planted in gardens for ornament since the foliage is lush and attractive. Kudzu quickly escaped from cultivation, romping through Georgia and nearby states and smothering huge tracts of land. It became known as the vine that ate the South, and now hardly anyone plants it.

Self-supporting by Rootlets, Holdfasts, or Tendrils with Discs

These vines will cling to anything, and it is from this list that one should select the vines for covering stone or brick work. Some grow more rampantly than others, some are evergreen and some are deciduous. None of them need be held to the building by man-made means of support.

Common Name	Scientific Name	Hardiness Zone
Trumpet creeper	*Campsis radicans*	4
Blood-trumpet vine	*Distictis buccinatoria*	10
Wintercreeper	*Euonymus fortunei*	5
Glossy wintercreeper	*Euonymus fortunei* 'Carrierei'	5
	Euonymus fortunei 'Gracilis'	5
Baby wintercreeper	*Euonymus fortunei* 'Minima'	5
Common wintercreeper	*Euonymus fortunei* radicans	5
Creeping fig	*Ficus pumila*	9
English ivy	*Hedera helix*	5
Gold-leaf ivy	*Hedera helix* 'Aureo-variegata'	5
Baltic ivy	*Hedera helix* 'Baltica'	5
Bunch-leaf ivy	*Hedera helix* 'Conglomerata'	5
Finger-leaf ivy	*Hedera helix* 'Digitata'	5
Small-leaf ivy	*Hedera helix* 'Minima'	5
Climbing hydrangea	*Hydrangea anomala petiolaris*	4
Catclaw vine	*Macfadyena unguis-cati*	8
St. Paul Virginia creeper	*Parthenocissus quinquefolia* 'Saint-paulii'	3
Japanese creeper or Boston-ivy	*Parthenocissus tricuspidata*	4
Low's Japanese creeper	*Parthenocissus tricuspidata* 'Lowii'	4
Veitch's Japanese creeper	*Parthenocissus tricuspidata* 'Veitchii'	4
Tanglehead	*Pileostegia viburnoides*	7
Japanese hydrangea-vine	*Schizophragma hydrangeoides*	5

George Taloumis

Dutchman's pipe *(Aristolochia durior)* covers a porch or trellis with sun-shading leaves after the unusual flowers have faded.

Twining Vines

The following are selected for twining up a rainspout, a wire, or for use on lattice work or on chain-link fences. Once given a good start they will take care of themselves, but some of them may grow so vigorously that they will have to be headed back from time to time. If the fence abuts the sidewalk, the long runners of bittersweet vines, for instance, can become a hazard to pedestrians. In such a case a close-clinging vine such as the fleece vine or the Virginia creeper would be better.

Common Name	Scientific Name	Hardiness Zone
Actinidias	*Actinidia* species	4, 7
Fiveleaf akebia	*Akebia quinata*	4
Dutchman's pipe	*Aristolochia durior*	4
Bittersweets	*Celastrus* species	2, 4
Carolina jessamine	*Gelsemium sempervirens*	7
Scarlet kadsura	*Kadsura japonica*	7
Honeysuckles	*Lonicera* species	3-5
Moonseed	*Menispermum canadense*	5
Wire vine	*Muehlenbeckia complexa*	6
Silk vines	*Periploca* species	5, 6
Silver fleece-vine	*Polygonum aubertii*	4
Chinese magnolia-vine	*Schisandra chinensis*	4
Himalayan magnolia-vine	*Schisandra propinqua*	8
Chinese star-jasmine	*Trachelospermum jasminoides*	7-8
Regel's threewingnut	*Tripterygium regelii*	4
Wisterias	*Wisteria* species	4, 5

Clinging by Means of Tendrils

These too can be used on lattice work and on chain-link fences; but they are not too satisfactory on single-wire supports, for they need something horizontal around which they can fasten their tendrils. The grapes are so vigorous that they are grown on horizontal wires in vineyards, but the home gardener frequently finds that he must assist them a bit during the growing season in order to guide vigorously growing shoots.

Common Name	Scientific Name	Hardiness Zone
Ampelopsis	*Ampelopsis* species	4, 7
Coralvine	*Antigonon leptopus*	9
Crossvine	*Bignonia capreolata*	6
Clematis	*Clematis* species (tendrils in the form of modified leaf stalks)	4, 5, 6
Cup-and-saucer vine	*Cobaea scandens*	9
Catclaw vine	*Macfadyena unguis-cati*	8
Silver vein creeper	*Parthenocissus henryana*	8
Virginia creeper	*Parthenocissus quinquefolia*	3
Engelmann Virginia creeper	*Parthenocissus quinquefolia* 'Engelmannii'	3
Passion flowers	*Passiflora* species	7-8
Silver fleece-vine	*Polygonum aubertii* (modified leaf stalks)	4
Summer grape	*Vitis aestivalis*	4
Glory vine grape	*Vitis coignetiae*	5
Doan grape	*Vitis doaniana*	6
Fox grape	*Vitis labrusca*	5
Riverbank grape	*Vitis riparia*	2
European grape	*Vitis vinifera*	6
Frost grape	*Vitis vulpina*	5

For Banks

Occasionally there are banks too steep for grass to be grown properly, and possibly too difficult or not important enough to plant with special ground covers. The vines in this list are the ones that can be expected to ramble over such banks, covering the soil and any rocks or holes that are present. As is stated in the accompanying articles, *Akebia quinata* and Hall's honeysuckle are so vigorous that they can get out of control and become serious pests, while *Euonymus obovata* is much slower in growth and is easily restrained. Usually English ivy is easily controlled, certainly in the North, but in the South it can become a rampant spreader. So, select from among the plants in this list with care, realizing in advance that it would probably be best to plant slow-spreading ground covers on the short bank and reserve the vines in this list for the very steep bank or the bank with poor sandy soil or the bank where anything is desirable that will cover the ground. It should also be pointed out that the memorial rose and Hall's honeysuckle are both excellent for their habit of rooting along their stems where they may touch moist soil, and so these aid materially in preventing soil erosion.

Common Name	Scientific Name	Hardiness Zone
Akebia	*Akebia* species	4
October clematis	*Clematis apiifolia*	4
Sweet autumn clematis	*Clematis dioscoreifolia robusta (paniculata)*	5
Travelers' joy	*Clematis vitalba*	4
Italian clematis	*Clematis viticella*	5
Big-leaf wintercreeper	*Euonymus fortunei vegeta*	5
Running euonymus	*Euonymus obovata*	3
English ivy	*Hedera helix*	5
Hall's Japanese honeysuckle	*Lonicera japonica* 'Halliana'	4
Moonseed	*Menispermum canadense*	5
Virginia creeper	*Parthenocissus quinquefolia*	3
Rambler rose,		
Memorial rose	*Rosa wichuraiana*	5
Grapes	*Vitis* species	2-6

J. Horace McFarland

Hall's honeysuckle gives low, dense cover with profuse, fragrant blooms. It is invasive in the South but has a role in northern and California gardens provided it can be contained.

Ground Covers

Several vines can be used as ground covers. Most of them are not neat in doing this and will quickly climb any shrub or tree near by. Although this may not be harmful, there are some situations where it is not desirable. Some, like *Vinca minor* and *Hedera helix,* will require little attention, and others, like the bittersweets, may quickly grow out of bounds and require a considerable amount of care to keep restrained. Therefore, vines as ground covers should be selected only after careful study of the situation.

Common Name	Scientific Name	Hardiness Zone
Fiveleaf akebia	*Akebia quinata*	4
Pepper-vine	*Ampelopsis arborea*	7
Bittersweets	*Celastrus* species	2, 4
Wintercreepers	*Euonymus fortunei* vars.	5
Running euonymus	*Euonymus obovata*	3
English ivy	*Hedera helix* vars.	5
Henry honeysuckle	*Lonicera henryi*	4
Hall's Japanese honeysuckle	*Lonicera japonica* 'Halliana'	4
Moonseed	*Menispermum canadense*	5
Wire vine	*Muehlenbeckia complexa*	6
Silver vein creeper	*Parthenocissus henryana*	8
Virginia creeper	*Parthenocissus quinquefolia*	3
Engelmann Virginia creeper	*Parthenocissus quinquefolia* 'Engelmannii'	3
St. Paul Virginia creeper	*Parthenocissus quinquefolia* 'Saint-paulii'	3
Kudzu vine	*Pueraria lobata*	6
Memorial rose	*Rosa wichuraiana*	5
Big periwinkle	*Vinca major*	7
Common periwinkle	*Vinca minor*	4

Withstanding Moist to Wet Soil

The wetter the soil, the more difficult it is to find plants that will grow. These are among the vines to be considered for a moist situation. If they do not grow well, there are probably none that will.

Common Name	Scientific Name	Hardiness Zone
Trumpet creeper	*Campsis radicans*	4
Virgin's bower	*Clematis virginiana*	4
Moonseed	*Menispermum canadense*	5
Chinese star-jasmine	*Trachelospermum jasminoides*	7-8

Sweet autumn clematis cascades with feathery flowers just when the trees are turning color. A robust grower with lustrous, semi-evergreen foliage, it sometimes escapes from gardens.

Withstanding Dry Soil

When the soil is very dry, there are only a few plants that will grow in it. When dry soil conditions are a problem, everything possible should be done to mix humus materials with the soil and to mulch the plants as well, in order that every bit of moisture be conserved. These are the vines that should be considered for such trying situations.

Common Name	Scientific Name	Hardiness Zone
Pepper-vine	*Ampelopsis arborea*	7
Trumpet creeper	*Campsis radicans*	4
October clematis	*Clematis apiifolia*	4
Scarlet clematis	*Clematis texensis*	5
Virgin's bower	*Clematis virginiana*	4
Creeping fig	*Ficus pumila*	9
Trumpet honeysuckle	*Lonicera sempervirens*	3
Virginia creeper	*Parthenocissus quinquefolia*	3
Japanese creeper	*Parthenocissus tricuspidata*	4
Silver fleece vine	*Polygonum aubertii*	4

Withstanding Shade

Actinidias	*Actinidia* species	4, 7
Fiveleaf akebia	*Akebia quinata*	4
Dutchman's pipe	*Aristolochia durior*	4
Clematis	*Clematis* species	4, 5, 6
Wintercreepers	*Euonymus fortunei* vars.	5
Running euonymus	*Euonymus obovata*	3
Carolina jessamine	*Gelsemium sempervirens*	7
English ivy	*Hedera helix* vars.	5
Climbing hydrangea	*Hydrangea anomala petiolaris*	4
Honeysuckles	*Lonicera* species	4-6
Moonseed	*Menispermum canadense*	5
	Parthenocissus species	3, 4, 8
Tanglehead	*Pileostegia viburnoides*	7
Japanese hydrangea-vine	*Schizophragma hydrangeoides*	5
Bengal clockvine	*Thunbergia grandiflora*	8
Chinese star-jasmine	*Trachelospermum jasminoides*	7-8
Grapes	*Vitis* species	2-6

Annual Vines

Annual vines have many uses in the garden. A few are treated as annuals in the North, but are more-or-less perennial in the deep South and in the Tropics. These are marked with an asterisk (*) in the following list:

*Cup-and-saucer vine	*Cobaea scandens*
Gourds	*Cucurbita, Lagenaria, Luffa*
Hyacinth-bean	*Dolichos lablab*
Hop vine	*Humulus japonicus*
Moonflower	*Ipomoea alba*
Scarlet starglory	*Ipomoea coccinea*
Cardinal-climber	*Ipomoea multifida*
Cypress vine	*Ipomoea quamoclit*
Morning-glories	*Ipomoea tricolor*
Sweet pea	*Lathyrus odoratus*
*Balsam-apple	*Momordica balsamina*
*Balsam-pear	*Momordica charanita*
*Clock vine	*Thunbergia alata*
Nasturtium	*Tropaeolum majus*
Canary-bird vine	*Tropaeolum peregrinum*

CARE OF ORNAMENTAL VINES

Given proper planting and training, vines can be an asset in any garden

Donald Wyman

It is of the utmost importance that the right kind of vine be selected for the right place. Vines are vigorous growers—they can easily outstrip all other woody plants in the length they grow each year. Some, like the kudzu vine (*Pueraria lobata*), can grow 30 to 50 feet in a single year! As a result, they can quickly cover wall or trellis space, but they can grow out of control just as quickly and create a great deal of extra work to keep them within the proper limits. So, a twining vine for a rainspout or trellis, a clinging vine for a stone wall or trellis, an evergreen clinging vine for the chimney, and a fruiting vine where it will show off to best advantage—all these are possibilities, but each situation should be given careful thought before the vine is finally selected.

Most vines can be expected to grow best in good garden soils. In the case of wisterias (as is explained on page 65) too good a soil may result in over-vigorous

vegetative growth and no flowers. For most of the vines grown for their foliage, this is not a special problem. Clematises are a bit difficult to grow well and present problems of their own, while the problems of growing rambler roses are sufficiently well known so that they need not be dealt with here.

Usually all vines will respond to a moderate amount of fertilizer by increased growth. However, they have individual methods of climbing and attaching themselves to supports. If one has a brick wall 20 feet high and 20 feet long, one plant of Boston-ivy could probably cover the wall eventually, but three or four vines spaced 5 feet apart would do the job much more quickly. Sometimes it is desired to have a trellis completely covered with vines to screen the viewer and to give shade. In such cases, vigorous-growing, large-leaved vines might be in order. It should be remem-

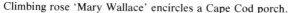
Climbing rose 'Mary Wallace' encircles a Cape Cod porch.

George Taloumis

49

Boston ivy *(Parthenocissus tricuspidata)* quickly covers a house or wall. As with most vines, some trimming may be necessary to keep it within bounds.

bered in this connection that not all vines grow as high or as dense as some. English ivy where it proves winter hardy, may grow to the top of the tallest tree yet not have the screening value of the larger-leaved Dutchman's pipe.

Training young vines need not be difficult. Once the purpose for which they have been selected has been decided, then comes the matter of training them to cover the trellis or wall properly. If they are to be tied to some support, the binding should not be too tight, otherwise it might strangle the plant. Vigorous pruning frequently results in increased elongation of the stems remaining, but it should be remembered that all in all the plant that is heavily pruned actually produces less leaf surface in the end.

It has been observed that sometimes a vine that is trained horizontally will produce more flowers than one growing vertically, although this may not always be the case. Pruning of any kind might best be done in the early spring except on certain of the vines such as some kinds of clematis and the wisterias, which are grown chiefly for their spring flowers.

A vigorous, tall-growing vine will frequently produce a major part of its leaves at the ends of the shoots, i.e., considerably above the ground, thus leaving the basal portion bare of leaves. In this case, a runner should be bent downward and around the bare portion of the plant. If the vine is growing more than is desired, pruning the roots may reduce the over-all growth quickly.

Clinging vines

Some of the clinging vines are very easy to start. Boston-ivy, for instance, quickly grows up a wall, fastening its small root-like holdfasts tenaciously to anything with which it comes in contact; and these hold the vine securely during the rest of its life. Some, such as the climbing hydrangea, are often difficult to start. This

50

George Taloumis

A young Japanese wisteria
blooms after the broadleaf
evergreens for continuing
color at the front door.

vine takes a year or so before it really begins to grow well. During that time the growth is slow and the small roots are not always able to hold the vine firmly to the wall. In this case, some support or system of tight wires should be used to hold the young shoots firmly against the wall; then it will not be long before the plant will be self-holding. An old climbing hydrangea on the three-story brick administration building at the Arnold Arboretum, once it was properly started, has never needed wires or any other means to hold it to the building in the forty-five years it has been growing there.

Some vines grow considerably faster than others, and this fact also should be taken into consideration when a variety is first being selected. Virginia creeper, for instance, will grow twice as fast as English ivy. Consequently, if only a very small area is to be covered by a clinging vine, like the side of a chimney on a shingle house, the English ivy might be the plant to select; although it would take a longer time for it to cover the chimney, it would not require the constant pruning and cutting back afterwards to keep it from spreading over the shingles on the remainder of the house. Boston-ivy is another vine which is excellent for clinging to stonework but should be used carefully on houses where it can get between shingles. This vine grows very vigorously, at least 6 to 10 feet each year, and must be cut back rigorously at least twice a year to restrain it from covering the house. It is far better to plant a slower-growing vine under such circumstances, especially on small areas, and so save a great deal of pruning later on.

Sometimes it becomes necessary to remove an old, established clinging vine from a wall, and many stems are broken or injured and cannot be replaced. In this case, especially if the vine is a vigorously growing one, it would be better to cut the vine down to the ground and let it start up again.

This pruning should be done in the very

early spring, not in the late summer or early fall. If work on the wall is to be done in the summer or fall, cut the vine down late in the spring and let it grow as it will along the ground until after the work on the wall is done. Then most of the young shoots can be attached to the wall. The difficulty in cutting down an old vine in the summer or early fall is that the new growth might not have a sufficient time to harden off before winter; it might be seriously injured, if not completely killed back, by that first winter.

Twining Vines

It is the twiners that really create problems. Most of these are vigorous growers and unless carefully watched they will grow out of line and attach themselves to any means of support within reach. In training them one should know, first of all, that they climb by twining in two different ways. Some climb by twining from left to right, as do the members of the following genera: *Actinidia, Akebia*, Dutchman's pipe (*Aristolochia*), bittersweet (*Celastrus*), moonseed (*Menispermum*), silk vine (*Periploca*), some of the native *Wisteria* species and Chinese wisteria (*W. sinensis*). Others, such as some of the species of honeysuckle (*Lonicera*), Chinese magnolia-vine (*Schisandra chinensis*), and Japanese wisteria (*W. floribunda*), climb by twining from right to left. By winding young runners around their supports in the right direction, one can shorten the time it takes them to become properly established.

Of course the trellis is the first place one has in mind for twining vines. Many types of trellises are available and such vines as Dutchman's pipe and honeysuckle are old-fashioned favorites long selected for this purpose. Trees are the poorest kind of support that can be used. Usually the tree trunk is too wide for a young twining vine to make a complete turn. The smallest wire is far more suitable. Bittersweet, akebia, wisteria, and bower actinidia are all vigorous twiners. The uninitiated gardener might think it would be a good idea to have a graceful vine high up in the branches of some tree—and it might, but not a twiner. Such

a vine can quickly strangle branches and trunks by completely encircling them, and so cause considerable damage to the tree.

There are times when a twining vine is wanted on the side of a house. This is certainly understandable for there is nothing quite as beautiful in the fall and early winter as a narrow column of fruiting bittersweet. Such a column can be grown by stretching a sturdy wire perpendicularly up the side of the house, preferably so attached that it is held several inches away from the wall. Bittersweet will quickly twine its way up such a support, especially if there are several horizontal "holds" for the vine, spaced 6 to 8 feet apart; once it grows up to these, it will twine itself around in such a way that it will not slide back to the base if heavy snow or ice places much weight on it in the winter. This type of support, too, is perfect for the shingle or clapboard house; when repainting time comes the entire wire need merely be removed and laid on the ground while the painting is being done. Later it can be replaced so that the length of the vine need not be shortened one bit by the painting operation. It is not too difficult to keep the vine restrained once it has reached the complete height desired, but it is important that it be not allowed to grow indiscriminately around the gutters and shingles. In so doing it can cause a real hazard by undermining the shingles; and it can produce a fire hazard by plugging up the gutters in such a way as to cause the collection of leaves there in the fall.

Wisteria is more difficult to handle; the vine usually has to grow several years before flowers are produced and cutting it to the ground every so often would keep it from producing flowers almost indefinitely.

Most vines are interesting to grow and reward the gardener surprisingly well for a little care. There are many places in every garden where vines can be grown to good advantage. If allowed to grow uncared for they can quickly become pests; but a little intelligent care at the right time, to keep them properly restrained, will make them real assets in any landscape or foundation planting. ❧

Akebia quinata

VINES ON WALLS
Which vines to use;
how to plant and care for them
Lyle L. Blundell

Clinging vines furnish their own trellises. All that is needed is a vertical surface; they will make themselves very much at home on tree trunks or on walls, whether masonry or wood. Here a precaution is in order. Vines crossing a shingled facade may add much to the picture, but when they are permitted to remain too long on wooden structures, especially in wet climates, the retention of moisture about the aerial roots makes preservation of wood difficult. It is safer to restrict clinging vines to brick or stone masonry, stucco, chimneys or rock walls.

Planting

Planting of these vines against a building wall is many times unrewarding and disappointing for several years. This is because soil at the bases of walls is generally the poorest encountered on a property. All manner of construction debris, with little or no good growing soil, is likely to be dumped back against the foundation as backfill; not until the roots have extended beyond this debris into the better soil well away from the foundation does the vine show any appreciable indication of covering the space provided for it. Thorough preparation of the soil is more important at the bases of walls on which vines are to be grown than anywhere else in the garden, because of the large leaf surface which it will be called on to nourish. When poor soil conditions are found, all soil and debris should be removed from a much larger hole than seems warranted by the root system planted. A hole 2 feet deep and 3 feet wide, extending to the undisturbed soil

Euonymus, trained up the pedestal and trimmed to maintain the underlying form. At right, a Japanese lantern com-ᵖˡemented by English ivy.

beyond the foundation excavation, is not too large. Backfill this planting area with good loam into which has been incorporated well-rotted manure to one-fourth of its volume. If manure is lacking, leaf mold or compost fortified with commercial fertilizer will suffice. If the soil is unduly heavy, sand should be incorporated to make it more friable. In such a soil the vine will quickly make the anticipated cover.

Training

No clinging vines, when well established and vigorous, are particular as to the surface over which they travel; therefore a severe pruning program will have to be carried on to keep them from wooden walls, windows and cornices, or otherwise held within bounds. Fortunately few of them are hurt by severe pruning.

Another means of growing vines against walls—one that maintains more automatic control of the area of coverage—is to place an iron pipe trellis or a wire or two against the wall (see page 58); on this support a twining vine such as bittersweet, honeysuckle or wisteria may be grown. For a low wall or a wooden house, a wooden trellis can be used. I recall one very effective garden retaining wall treatment. The wall was covered with common wintercreeper for winter richness; outside of this, about a foot from the wall surface, was an open wooden trellis which carried climbing roses for summer floral display.

Some vines are planted essentially for the beauty of their foliage. This is especially true of wall vines. The beauty and character of the plant is largely governed by the richness and texture of the foliage. The side of a large building can very adequately take a large, fast-growing, coarse vine, whereas a small garden requires a richer, finer-textured plant.

Euonymus

Evergreen vines have the richest foliage and generally are the most refined in growth and appearance; wintercreeper (*Euonymus fortunei*) and English ivy

(Hedera helix) can surpass many deciduous vines in wall coverage. (For comments on English ivy, see pp.14, 77). Evergreen vines are broad-leaf plants and in the North are frequently subject to late winter foliage burn caused by excessive loss of water from the leaves when the ground is frozen and moisture cannot be replaced. This burning can be reduced to the minimum if evergreens are restricted to north and east exposures. Never plant an evergreen vine on a southwest exposure, where the burning is most severe because of the drying afternoon sun.

The smallest and most refined of the evergreen climbers is the baby wintercreeper *(Euonymus fortunei* 'Minima'). This miniature variation of the wintercreeper, with leaves the size of one's little fingernail, seldom grows over 3 feet high, and actually does not cling but will grow erect against a wall, tree trunk, or garden ornament. This is a choice miniature for an intimate spot on a low wall. It is one vine that rarely needs pruning.

The common wintercreeper *(Euonymus fortunei radicans)* is more robust, but may take many years to reach 10 or 15 feet high. It clings by rootlets, so crevices in the wall help its anchorage. The leaves are an inch long, oval, deep green, some of them more or less streaked with white.

Grown in deep shade, this plant will probably change very little in form in many years, but when given a freer growing location, within a few years the plant changes in character. Large branches grow horizontally from the wall; the leaves become larger and glossier, the buds are larger, and small green flowers and tan and orange fruits are produced in clusters on these branches. This mature form is known to the gardener as the glossy wintercreeper *(Euonymus fortunei* 'Carrierei'). The over-zealous growth extending from a building wall may catch high winds and the whole vine may be pulled to the ground. The horizontal branches can be cut back to half their length, thereby reducing the wind leverage, and the whole surface of the plants can be made neater by this shearing. A wire stretched along the wall will give added support.

Similar to the glossy wintercreeper, but with slightly larger, round, and less shiny leaves (about the size of a half-dollar), is the big-leaf wintercreeper *(Euonymus fortunei vegeta)*. The flowers are produced freely and are small and greenish; the fruits which follow, dangling clusters of orange berries in creamy husks, remain throughout the winter. From the appearance of these fruits the plant is often called the evergreen bittersweet. While these two fruiting forms of wintercreeper are usually propagated by cuttings, the seeds can be planted and will produce the juvenile, or nonfruiting, forms. The seedlings of the big-leaf wintercreeper are round-leaved, small and a very soft dark green. This variation seems to have been overlooked, as I have never seen a name assigned to it. I recommend these big-leaf seedlings for a rich vine or ground cover.

One other important variety, the purple-leaf wintercreeper *(Euonymus fortunei* 'Colorata'), seems not to develop rootlets. I have only once seen it take to a wall enthusiastically, and this was with the aid of the gutter downspout.

All wintercreepers are attacked by a serious insect pest known as the euonymus scale. This insect makes more than one brood a year—the hotter the weather the greater the number of broods—so that a small infestation can spread rapidly in the course of a year. Control is difficult when the insect is well established. (See page 60.)

Deciduous Vines

Deciduous clinging vines have compensating characters which make up for their lack of foliage in winter. The blaze of color on the creepers in the fall makes this season their most outstanding, and

Both photos, George Taloumis

Above, climbing hydrangea (*H. anomala petiolaris*) in bloom on north side of house; below, woodbine or Virginia creeper (*Parthenocissus quinquefolia*) cascades down a seashore foundation.

the flowers on the climbing hydrangeas add to their spring attractiveness.

The smallest-textured plant among deciduous vines is Low's Japanese creeper (*Parthenocissus tricuspidata* 'Lowii'). Used on low walls or at an entrance, it decorates without dominating. The leaves are only about an inch across, several pointed, and curled; they have short stalks so that the growth stays close to the wall. The holdfasts are not so well developed as those of *P. tricuspidata*. This vine produces no fruit but its fall color is a brilliant red.

Japanese creeper (*Parthenocissus tricuspidata*), also called Boston-ivy, although it is a native of Japan and China, is the most generally useful of all clinging vines. It attaches itself to the wall at first by "sticky fingers"—branched tendrils with enlarged disks at the ends of the branches; as it grows, the larger stems develop aerial roots which hold more firmly. The leaf somewhat resembles that of English ivy and here, as in English ivy, there are two plants in one. As the new growth starts out from the root, spreading in all directions, the leaves are small (less than an inch across), and sometimes purple and divided into three parts when young. As the plant develops, the leaves become larger; along the older stems the flower spurs develop—leaves here may be 4 to 8 inches across on stems a foot long.

The young, or juvenile, stage of the plant, with small leaves, has given rise to a variety named Veitch's Japanese creeper (*Parthenocissus tricuspidata* 'Veitchii'). If one wishes to keep this character, the vine can be pulled from the wall periodically, so that it will send out its new delicate tracery across the face of the wall. But when given free rein, this vine is a vigorous wall covering and has no concern for windows in its path. It is not particular about soil, and is most useful in covering large blank walls as it becomes larger in scale with its own maturity. The bees find that this plant furnishes a great supply of midsummer nectar from its greenish flowers, and the clumps of blue berries that follow add to the picture in the fall after the gorgeous scarlet leaves

Low's Boston-ivy has rosette-like leaves about an inch across. It is attractive
in containers and small gardens, or as tracery along a stucco wall.

drop. The berries are persistent; and for those of us in the North another interesting picture is produced as the wet snow clings to the fruit spurs in an interesting pattern of blue and white against a wall.

The native Virginia creeper *(Parthenocissus quinquefolia)*, sometimes also known locally as woodbine, is not so successful as a wall vine. It is even bolder in its foliage effect, but neither the disks that stick the plant to the wall nor the aerial roots are so well developed as in the Japanese creeper. Certain varieties, particularly 'Saint-paulii', are said to cling more closely, but the best recommendation for these vines is to have a very rough surfaced wall or wires attached for support. Otherwise the plant will come plunging down in a year or two.

The leaves of Virginia creeper are five-parted and vary in size from a few inches across near the end of the stem to more than a foot across along the older stems. The shoots tend to grow vertically, spreading less broadly than those of the Japanese creeper; so for a complete cover, plants must be planted more closely. The various shades of red make the plant one of the most brilliant in the fall landscape. The blue berries, the size of a small pea, are borne in open clusters and either fall before winter or are eaten by the birds after the leaves drop.

Another "almost holding" vine is the trumpet creeper *(Campsis radicans)*. This vine clings with the aid of a few rootlets at each joint; and unless given the aid of a gutter downspout or a chance crevice, it will be pulled down by the wind, which whips the large free-growing branches. Although usually used as a trellis vine, I have seen it attach itself, climb a two-story house, go up the roof, and seem to look for further heights after reaching the top of the chimney. The foliage is not very rich, being similar in appearance to ash leaves. The gorgeous orange or red trumpet-shaped flowers, 3 inches long in terminal clusters, are the great triumph of this vine, and the rather thick cigar-like fruit pods on the bright tan stems add to its winter interest.

The coarsest of all self-attaching vines are two related plants, the climbing hydrangea *(Hydrangea anomala petiolaris)* and the Japanese hydrangea-vine *(Schizophragma hydrangeoides)*. These plants are so coarse that they are satisfactory only on the largest and coarsest of stone work, where they are happily in scale. Both of these vines cling by rootlets and thrust out from the wall branches 1 to 3 feet long, on which the leaves and flowers are borne.

Opinions differ as to which of these vines is to be preferred, most authorities recommending the climbing hydrangea. My own preference is for Japanese hydrangea-vine; I like its sharply saw-toothed, smaller leaves, as well as its shorter branches and habit of remaining closer to the wall. ❧

57

VINES ON BUILDINGS
And methods of attaching them
Milton Baron

In planning the use of vines on buildings, esthetic aims must be balanced against practical considerations. Vines, like other plant materials, used astutely, enhance the architecture by interesting line, foliage pattern, and in certain cases, flowers. Poor features of the building's exterior may be hidden and the harshness of large areas of brick or masonry be relieved. When there is little room for trees or shrubs, as is frequently the case in our cities, vines can be used on buildings even if there is only so much as a square foot of soil for planting. The arrangement of planting pockets must be decided upon prior to laying concrete or asphalt surfaces. Besides growing in restricted areas, many vines tolerate adverse conditions such as the deep shade of north exposures, city atmosphere, and low soil fertility. Years ago it was thought most climbers were slow in starting. This has been disproved by giving reasonable care to vines planted in pockets of well prepared, enriched soil. Certain species will grow six or more feet the first year, far exceeding the increment of other woody materials for the same period.

As a result of this rapid growth, certain vines may become too large for their location or too heavy for their supports. Occasional vigorous pruning may be necessary to keep growth within proper bounds. When too many vines are planted, or if allowed to grow without restrictive pruning, even window screens will be covered by a heavy matting of green. No control except pruning in the early summer seems to check this. Reduction of the vine mass also cuts down on roosting places for birds.

Fortunately, vines are easy to maintain. In general, they are subject to but few insects or diseases; as a group their care is no greater, and in many cases is less, than that of trees or shrubs. Should minimum upkeep be desired, proper selection of the species at the start is all-important.

Since vines climb in several ways, this charactertistic is most important. Vines which climb and adhere by means of rootlets or tendrils with discs (see page 44) support themselves as they grow and are perhaps the most practical to use. They should be used only on structures or walls of stone or masonry. If used on wood, they cannot be easily removed when

All drawings, William J. Johnson

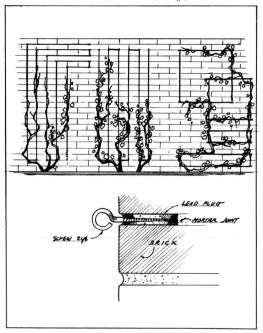

Vine supports of galvanized or braided wire fastened with hooks or screw eyes are not obvious to the observer.

Wooden vine supports are useful for displaying climbers up a clapboard house. They should be designed to harmonize with the architecture of the building. Attach with metal angles for easy maintenance.

painting is needed, and they have a tendency to damage the surface and wood itself. Wooden structures are best clothed by vines separated from the wall surfaces to allow air circulation and easy maintenance. To accomplish this the choice should be from the group which twines about a support or which climb by means of tendrils (see page 45). These must be provided with means of climbing support, otherwise they make an unsightly heap or trail aimlessly on the ground. ❧

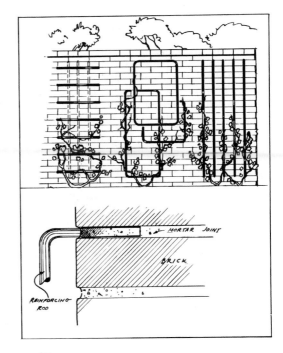

The most permanent kinds of vine supports are made of wrought iron or reinforcing rods. They form a definite pattern against the wall or building.

EUONYMUS SCALE

About the only vine pests causing any serious difficulty in the northern and central part of the country are the scale insects, chiefly attacking *Euonymus* and sometimes the bittersweets. Euonymus scale especially causes much injury over widespread areas. This pest was introduced into America from the Orient prior to 1880 when it was first discovered in this country at Norfolk, Virginia. Since that time it has spread widely both in the United States and Canada, although it must be admitted that at present the pest seems to be more difficult in the eastern and northeastern parts of the country than it is elsewhere.

Life History

Euonymus scale not only infests species of *Euonymus* but sometimes is found on the varieties of the common lilac, bittersweet, pachysandra and English ivy *(Hedera)*. The treatment or control is the same in each case. Most of the small white scales that are seen are the males, which are very small and narrow, while the females are larger, wider and light brown, and consequently not so easily seen at the first glance.

When the crawlers first emerge from the egg in the spring they move around on the plant for 12 to 36 hours, and then they settle and remain in one spot. They may crawl anywhere from ⅛ inch to 16 inches during that period. It takes about 46 days for the scale to mature, and in the vicinity of Massachusetts there are two generations a year. They spend the winter either as a mature or immature fertilized female. Their life history is definitely dependent on the weather, for in one year with a cool late spring, crawlers were not noticed near Boston until June 15th while in another section with warmer weather they appeared June 1st. It is essential to keep this in mind when determining the time to spray.

Control

No half measures will control euonymus scale; it can seriously injure and actually kill well-established vines if allowed to go unchecked. Sometimes it may be necessary to cut the vines to the ground, spray the remaining stubs thoroughly and so start the plant all over again, in order to control the pest properly.

In late March or early April, apply "Superior"-type dormant spray, 60- or 70-sec. oil with or without ethion. Follow manufacturer's directions. To control crawlers, spray in early to midspring with carbaryl (Sevin) or a multipurpose spray containing malathion and methoxychlor. The number of applications for crawlers depends on the amount of infestation and the weather. Applications should be made ten to fourteen days apart in two or three applications. A well-grown, scale-free planting of *Euonymus* is very much worth a little attention now and then. ❧

Left: female scale insect; center, male; right, infested euonymus branch showing more males (white) than females. Dotted areas on leaves represent normal green; white areas the yellowing effect of infestation.

Eva Melady

VINES WITH SEXES SEPARATE
Male plants never fruit; female plants fruit if males are sufficiently near

Donald Wyman

There are at least five kinds of vines with sexes separate—that is, with the pollen-bearing (male) flowers on one plant and the pistil-bearing (female) flowers on another plant. It is only these pistillate flowers that develop into fruits, and usually they do so only if a male plant is in the near vicinity to supply the pollen. The five genera of vines in this group are *Actinidia*, *Celastrus* (bittersweet), *Schisandra*, *Smilax* (cat brier) and, occasionally, *Vitis* (grape).

From the standpoint of ornament, the bittersweets are the most important of all; because of their bright orange fruits they are among the most popular of all fruiting vines. Many people have been disappointed because carefully grown bittersweet vines, in a prominent garden spot, have never borne fruits over the years. This has been either because a male (or staminate-flowering) vine was planted—which will never have fruits under any circumstances; or because a pistillate (or potentially fruiting) vine has been planted, with no near-by source of pollen from male plants to fertilize the pistillate flowers when they are in bloom.

We have experimented with bagging these flowers when they bloom and we know that in the case of bittersweet at least, pollen is necessary for fruiting. Experiments at the Arnold Arboretum have shown that pollen from male plants is carried by the wind or by insects nearly a quarter of a mile, though how much farther we do not know. There are three possibilities available to the homeowner to insure the fruiting of his bittersweet vine, provided of course, he has bought a

Flowers of actinidia: left, male; right, female. (Gundersen, *Families of Dicotyledons,* copyright 1950 Chronica Botanica Co.)

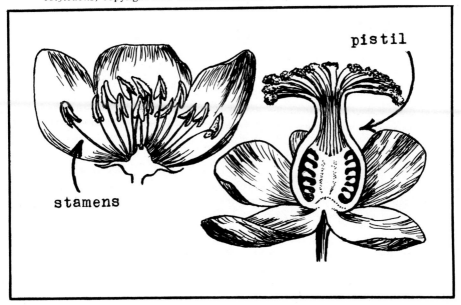

pistil

stamens

vine that either has fruit on it or is guaranteed to be a fruiting plant.

1. A small male plant can be planted in the same hole with the fruiting plant. This will have to be kept restrained somewhat, over the years, so that it does not grow more vigorously than the fruiting plant.

2. When the vine begins to flower, a bunch of branches with pollen-bearing flowers can be collected from the wild or from a known male plant, placed in a bottle of water, and hung up high in the pistillate vine. Wind and insects will do the rest, but the flowers should be in good condition for several days at least. I have done this very successfully, but the trick is to obtain the right flowers at just the right time. They usually bloom about June 10 in the vicinity of Boston.

3. The best way of all for gardeners with talent for experimentation is to bud graft a few buds from a staminate plant on the fruiting plant. This this easily done, with a little practice, after reading about budding in any well illustrated book on plant propagation (see BBG *Handbook on Propagation, pp. 25-28;* it should be done in August. Of course the branches that develop from such buds should be clearly marked so that they will not be pruned off. It may well be that scions could be grafted on the fruiting plant in the early spring instead, but the budding is simple and easily done.

The fruits of the bower actinidia (*A. arguta*) are not ornamental, hence are not desired unless one is interested in making preserves from them. If fruits are desired, the same possibilities are open as for bittersweet.

Magnolia-vine *(Schisandra)* has very attractive fruits (red, in pendulous clusters), but it is rarely used in this part of the country. The Chinese species, which is hardy here, bears its fruits well hidden by foliage, so that it is really not considered a desirable fruiting ornamental.

Smilax, because of its many thorns, is seldom planted as an ornamental.

Most of the grapes *(Vitis)*, especially the ones grown for their fruits, have both kinds of flowers on the same plant. A few of the species grown for ornament have sexes separate, but in these cases the fruits are not usually desirable.

It should be specifically noted that wisterias are definitely not in this group. They sometimes fail to flower and fruit for other reasons; but their flowers are perfect, and all wisteria vines should eventually bear the flowers to which we are accustomed. ✄

Poison-Ivy

This too is a vine but unlike most of the others, poison-ivy *(Rhus radicans)* is one we are always trying to eradicate. A vigorous grower, it will spread over anything and grow up the first upright object it reaches by attaching its small areial roots tenaciously to the means of support. Even at the seashore it grows within reach of salt water spray. Its autumn color is a rich orange and red. The compound leaves, made up of three parts, should be familiar to everyone, and its small white berries should also be just as well known. Unfortunately they are not! One winter, in a Boston suburb, some energetic garden club ladies included these "new berries we found in the woods" in some excellent Christmas wreaths, only to spend the vacation days uncomfortably realizing what it was they had used.

Chemical sprays can eradicate poison-ivy if used at the right time and according to manufacturer's directions. Use a non-selective herbicide with caution and discretion. Wet leaves thoroughly. Keep spray away from desirable plants. Ammonium sulfamate (Ammate) or Silvex, in areas of the country where it can be purchased, may also be used, but it must be remembered to keep this "brush killer" away from ornamental trees and shrubs in the garden. In the case of either spray, apply only on calm days, and be especially aware of runoff problems on slopes. ✄

A rampant grower, poison-ivy can be a lush, attractive vine, especially in autumn when it turns a splendid red or yellow. Its most familiar look is that of the modest-sized leaves at bottom left. Bottom right shows leaves and fruits contrasted with Virginia creeper, another vine that often appears in the same range but is harmless.

FLOWERING IN WISTERIA
Why wisteria may fail to flower and some pointers on what to do about it
Harold O. Perkins and Donald Wyman

Wisteria stands out from all the other vines as sometimes proving the most troublesome to bring into flower. Horticulturists receive many a query about vines that are ten to fourteen years old and have "never flowered." Some ask about the sexes of the plants, and others about where to buy plants guaranteed to flower. The answers to these questions are not as simple as they might be, but here are a few pointers about wisteria.

Sex Separation Not a Factor

Each flower of wisteria is hermaphroditic (both sexes present in the same flower); there is no such thing as separate male and female wisteria vines (as there is, for example, in bittersweet). Moreover, this factor affects only fruit production, not blossoming, so in any event it would not affect the ability of wisteria to bloom. Given the right conditions, all wisterias should flower. Admittedly the fact is that some of them fail to do so for many years, if ever.

Age of the Plant

In some cases all that may be necessary is to wait a few years; wisterias often take about seven years to reach a flowering

George Taloumis

With age wisteria forms a handsome, gnarled trunk that can attain the girth of a medium-sized tree. Because plants can live to a great age, it is a pity not to have flowers. For example, a century-old specimen near an entrance to Prospect Park in Brooklyn has probably never flowered despite lush vegetative growth.

Young wisteria, trained up a trellis and properly cultivated, is a breathtaking late spring sight. Plants tolerate city conditions well and the foliage is attractive during the growing season.

stage. In one instance a Japanese and a Chinese wisteria grew side by side. The Chinese vine bloomed beautifully every year, according to the owner, but the Japanese vine had never bloomed. At the time they were observed the Chinese vine was covered with flowers and a short time later the Japanese vine also had a few flowers. The owner said this was the first time in fifteen years that it had bloomed, but it might have bloomed sparsely before, unnoticed.

Over-fertilization

Heavy fertilizing, and especially an excess of nitrogen, results in heavy stem and leaf growth. This discourages flower bud formation. A plant which has an abundance of dark-colored, healthy foliage should, therefore, receive a no-nitrogen fertilizer, or no fertilizer at all.

Fertilizing with superphosphate is permissible and often desirable. A good way

WISTERIA MAY NOT FLOWER BECAUSE:

1) Plant is not old enough
2) Too rich soil (too much nitrogen) leads to excessive stem and leaf growth but no flowers
3) Winter cold (in northern areas) may kill flower buds
4) Root and top growth are out of balance
5) Insufficient sunlight

TO HELP INDUCE FLOWERING:

1) Wait a few years
2) Do not apply nitrogen fertilizers; apply superphosphate
3) Protect by taking down and covering in winter
4) Prune branches severely; root prune
5) Do not plant in shade

to do this is to dig a 2-foot trench about the base of the plant and mix a considerable amount of superphosphate with the soil as it returned to the trench.

Root Pruning

Applying superphosphate as above described serves a dual purpose. It supplies the feeding roots with an excess of phosphoric acid which may hasten flowering, and in the same operation it accomplishes root pruning. The latter may also be carried out by forcing a sharp spade into the soil in a circle about 18 inches from the trunk, thus cutting all the side roots.

Branch Pruning

If a plant shows excessive growth vigor, *i.e.,* rapid production of stems and leaves, the long shoots may be pruned back to two or three buds in the late spring. Repeat this pruning every other week until growth stops. This may help but is not a sure cure.

Climate

In the colder areas of the United States and southern Canada severe winters can kill flower buds, so that no amount of pruning or proper fertilizing will help flower production. In such places the vines should be taken down for the winter and covered with hay, brush, or soil, as is commonly recommended for rambler roses.

There is some evidence that sunlight is essential for flowering, so do not plant wisteria in the shade.

Purchasing Plants

Some commercial growers believe that certain clones are notably good flowering specimens and they always propagate from these. It is well to buy such plants, if available. Other nurseymen tie a knot in the young stem and claim that by so doing they make the vine certain to flower. Potted plants that have already flowered are sometimes available. ✄

Chinese vs. Japanese Wisteria

When wisteria is mentioned, most people think of the short-clustered Chinese wisteria *(W. sinensis)*, which is widely planted throughout the country, while only a few consider the hardier Japanese wisteria *(W. floribunda)*. Both have been in America about a century, but the Chinese plant has proved more popular. The flower clusters are about 7 to 14 inches long and all the flowers open simultaneously, making a beautiful display. The clusters of the Japanese vine may be 8 to 52 inches long (depending on the variety and the soil and moisture conditions where they are growing), and the individual flowers do not all open at once. Instead, the flowers begin to open at the base of the cluster and open progressively to the tip, so that usually not all the flowers in a cluster are in good condition at one time.

The Japanese vine makes up for this, however, in having some garden varieties (such as *W. floribunda* 'Macrobotrys') with clusters over 3 feet long. We have actually measured some at the Arnold Arboretum and found them to be 36 inches long. Then, too, the Japanese plant is hardier and has many varieties in the trade, one with pink flowers *(W. floribunda* 'rosea') and several with white flowers; still others have flowers varying slightly in size and color. The Japanese varieties can usually be distinguished from the Chinese in that they have thirteen to nineteen leaflets, while the Chinese has seven to thirteen leaflets.

Both types are splendid, vigorous-growing ornamental vines making wonderful displays when well grown. Selections should be made with the respective merits of each form clearly in mind. ✄

George Taloumis

Above is Chinese, below is Japanese wisteria. The former's blooms appear simultaneously, the latter's in sequence down a raceme that can be over three feet long.

ANNUAL CLIMBERS
How to grow some of these useful and attractive vines
Alys Sutcliffe

Most people are familiar with morning-glories as annual vines that grow quickly and flower prolifically if grown in a sunny place. They are useful plants to cover an unsightly fence or a bare wall.

There are several other annual vines which may be used for this purpose. They are easy to grow, some more so than others, and they usually flower well if planted in a sunny position. Some prefer rich soil with plenty of fertilizer and water, but some actually grow better in poor soils. This means that anyone can grow one or two annual vines that will flower most of the summer and fall until frost.

The following list of these vines and their culture may be helpful to the new homeowner with a wire fence or garage wall that he would like to beautify until some perennial vines are established.

Canary-bird vine *(Tropaeolum peregrinum)* has attractively cut leaves and yellow flowers, and will grow well in shady places. Seed can be sown out-of-doors when the ground is warm.

Nasturtium *(Tropaeolum majus)*. The climbing varieties of the garden nasturtium will grow in full sun in any sandy or gravelly soil, preferring this to a rich, heavy mixture. They should be sown out-of-doors as soon as the ground warms up a bit. Black aphids will infest them unless they are sprayed regularly with nicotine sulphate or some equally effective trade-name spray; even soapy water helps to keep them free of these pests.

The morning-glory family includes several species that have well-known climbers among them, including the obnoxious bind-weeds *(Convolvulus arvensis and C. sepium)*. Do not plant these!

J. Horace McFarland

Cardinal climber, an illustration of the usefulness of annual vines for providing quick cover.

Turk's cap, one of the larger, showier annual gourds.

J. Horace McFarland

The following are worthwhile vines:

Cardinal-climber (*Ipomoea* x *multifida*) is a strong and rapid grower with bright red flowers and fern-like foliage. Sowing can be done out-of-doors about the beginning of May. The seed should first be soaked in water for a few hours.

Moonflower (*Ipomoea alba*), a night-blooming morning-glory, has large, white, sweet-scented flowers that open in the early evening and fade towards morning. Although it is perennial in the tropics, it is treated as an annual in the North. There is a pink variety, also.

There are several very good varieties of morning-glories *(Ipomoea)* including 'Giant Cornell' with large red flowers that have a white border; 'Pearly Gates' a white variety; and 'Darling', wine-red with a white throat. 'Scarlett O'Hara' and 'Heavenly Blue' are old favorites. Clarke's early-flowering variety of 'Heavenly Blue' might come into flower sooner than often happens with morning-glories. All make plenty of strong growth and cover a fence quickly, but do not flower until late summer. Once they begin, they go on until frost. This is all right if you are away most of the summer and come home to find plenty of color in your garden, but it is disappointing if you plant morning-glories in your summer garden and have them start to flower just as you are about to leave at the end of the season.

Purple-bell cobaea or the cup-and-saucer vine or cathedral bells *(Cobaea scandens)* is a rapid-growing vine with purple bell-shaped flowers. The seeds are flat and should be put into the ground edge-wise. In the South this is perennial.

Hop-vine *(Humulus japonicus)* will make a quick cover for a fence. The leaves are quite handsome. There is also a white-variegated form grown from seeds.

Gourds for ornament are popular because they can be used for winter decorations. Most of them will grow over any garden fence. They need good soil, plenty of water and well-balanced fertilizer. The seed may be sown as soon as all danger of frost is over. When the plants begin to grow, a mulch will help to keep the roots cool and moist. The fruits should not be picked until the shells are hard, then they should be cut off with as much stem as possible. Wash the gourds with a soft brush dipped in some phenol disinfectant such as Lysol or Sylpho-Naphthol and leave them to dry. In three or four days they may be waxed or varnished.

Sweet pea *(Lathyrus odoratus)*. We are always hopeful that these will be worth the trouble they take, but except in special situations and for unexplainable reasons, they seldom are. For those who can succeed with them, they are superb annual climbers. They lend color and fra-

69

grance to the garden and are fine for cutting. They need a deeply-trenched rich soil and cool weather. In the fall dig a trench about 18 inches deep, put 9 inches of well-rotted manure in the bottom, and over this put 6 inches of good soil into which a complete fertilizer has been mixed. Sow the seed in November and cover with about 2 inches of soil; then fill the trench in with a light mulch of leaves or evergreen branches which can be removed in the spring. Sweet peas need plenty of water and should be picked daily; once they go to seed the vines soon begin to turn yellow.

General Tips on Culture

To get an early start, morning-glories and other annual vines may be sown in pots indoors. It is preferable to use some of the treated pots now on the market; these can be put into the ground, plants and all, without disturbing the roots. Use a light, porous soil and soak the seeds before sowing. They should not be sown out-of-doors until the soil is warm. As soon as, or even before, the seeds start to grow, it is important to have something for the vines to climb on so that there is no chance of their getting bent and broken. This is often the cause of failure with annual vines and is easily remedied by putting twigs in the pots or around the plants until they reach the fence or lattice over which they will eventually climb. ❧

The Unusual Flowers and Fruits of *Akebia quinata*

This interesting twiner from central China, Korea, and Japan is one of the best of the foliage vines in the North. The flowers, appearing in midspring, are not conspicuous but are most interesting. The pistillate (female) flowers have three purple petals ½ to 1 inch in diameter, with several conspicuous pistils in the center. The staminate (male) flowers are much smaller, practically all stamens. Often the staminate and the pistillate flowers are borne in the same loose pendulous cluster, about 4 inches long. Wind and insects in this country do not seem to be very effective in pollination. In certain areas fruits may result without human aid, but to insure the set of fruit, hand pollination must be resorted to at just the right time.

When this is done properly, the fleshy pods will develop by fall. These are purple, about 3 inches long, and filled with a mucilaginous material and many black seeds. These thick pods are useless, but the plant and its method of fruiting offer an excellent opportunity to observe sex in flowers and to do hand pollinating with results. ❧

Roche

Flowers of *Akebia quinata*—the large one is female, the small ones are male.

VINES OF THE SOUTH
Many varieties of fine climbing plants can be grown in warm climates
Roger B. Thompson

Vines seem to be more expressive of the tropical exuberance of nature than do trees, whose stature and incidence are everywhere within comparatively narrow limits. The farther one travels into the warmer and moister portions of our country, the more numerous are the vines one encounters, the more numerous the species, and the larger they become. The liana-choked tropics are no myth.

Vines in the North are, if not always docile, at least temperate and rather easily controlled. In more favorable circumstances of temperature, moisture, and length of growing season these same species sometimes graduate (or degenerate, depending upon one's interest in luxuriance or control) into predatory monsters, hydra-headed and menacing beyond belief; and all have relatives.

I have never been sympathetic with those who complain about the common and expected problems of maintenance; but when a man can go through a planting with a ditchbank blade (one of the most

lethal weapons ever placed in the hands of man—a wide, 18-inch, hookbilled piece of steel extended by a 3-foot handle) and return a week later to find his labors all undone, one can appreciate his wish that certain vines, at least, did not grow quite so rapidly.

Vines as a class are singularly free from insect pests in the southern states, though with notable exceptions. Scale insects make any attempt to grow *Euonymus fortunei* and its varieties a constant war, often brought to desperate termination by a steel instrument or a concentration of oil spray "guaranteed to kill."

Wisteria in the North requires its pruning, but here in the South it grows interminably. I once saw an entire yard fenced with a single plant. The owner had trained it over an arch above his front walk, and thence along a single strand of wire across the tops of forked cypress posts; it encircled his property like a python. Another with a trunk as thick as my body hung upon a massive live oak, enveloping

George Taloumis

Carolina jessamine (*Gelsemium sempervirens*) is extremely fragrant and, with butter-yellow flowers, very decorative in cultivation.

71

J. Horace McFarland

Cypress vine *(Ipomoea quamoclit)* has tiny scarlet and, in cultivars, white flowers. Originally tropical, it has found the American South quite congenial, and has naturalized there.

it almost to the tips of its twigs—the only tree with enough vitality to withstand its competition.

Both the cypress vine *(Ipomoea quamoclit)* and the scarlet starglogy *(I. coccinea),* annuals introduced from the tropics, have found the climate to their liking and run wild, tangling old cotton patches along with their small-flowered native relatives. An old field is often alive with their tiny scarlet stars amongst the more subdued pink, white and blue of related species.

In the far South the fingerleaf morning-glory *(Ipomoea digitata)*, a perennial, is one of the giants of its genus. Several thick succulent stems arise from a tuber to a height of 20 feet or more, bearing widely spaced five- or seven-fingered leaves broader than a man's hand. Flowers often as much as 3 inches across, rosy pink with deeper throats, are borne many in a cluster over a long period. Since, like other tuberous-rooted vines, it may be grown in the North by storage of its

tubers over winter, the range of this attractive vine should be liberally extended.

Yellow jessamine or Carolina jessamine *(Gelsemium sempervirens)*, often popularly called "jasmine," though widely distributed, seems not to be extensively cultivated. It is the state flower of South Carolina, and grows wild along the woods edge, twining and rambling over the bushes. We often come upon it in the midst of the forest, where it has grown up with the trees, unsuspected except when its fragrance permeates the whole woodland or its fallen yellow trumpets carpet the forest floor. Even then the cable-like stem, often hanging free from the high branches, may give the only clue to its precise whereabouts. Many have planted it with little success—shade for its roots, abundant water, and perhaps a nearly neutral soil being necessities.

Firecracker vine *(Manettia cordifolia)* is a tender vine which never gets out of hand, twining only to the eaves of a single-story house. Cut down by frost each year, it is hardy only where the ground never freezes; but its small, shining leaves make a very pleasing foliage mass, and the abundant, tubular, red flowers (1½ inches long and produced over a long season) make it a very attractive addition. It.is one of the few South Americans on our list.

Coralvine *(Antigonon leptopus)* is one of the best-loved of all southern vines, and one of the most widely distributed. So tender as to be cut to the ground by frost as a matter of course, we find it in midsummer covering the verandas along whole streets and smothering entire fronts of houses. The usual color of its small flowers, garlanded like beads, is bright rosy pink; but when the white form is also present in a neighborhood, seedlings of any tint betwixt the two may be locally common. Climbing by tendrils, it loops and sags, and having reached the top of its support cascades down again before regaining its hold; so it is often covered with bloom from top to bottom.

Crossvine *(Bignonia capreolata)* is very spectacular on the edges of woodlands in May, where its massed trumpets cover small trees like a thrown blanket, but it is not generally accepted for cultivation. Its blooming season is short and quickly over; one day it is in glory and next morning, after a little rain, its crown is in the mire.

More Rampant Vines

The Trumpet creeper *(Campsis radicans)* not much planted in the South except by those who use it to attract humming birds through the long, hot weeks of summer. Perhaps its rampant growth is not in its favor; but there is often prejudice against common things, especially those cherished by simple folk, who, never having known affluence, almost universally respond in a direct, impulsive way toward beauty without questioning its rarity or price.

Another of the bignonia family, catclaw vine *(Macfadyena unguis-cati,* formerly *Doxantha unguis-cati),* hardy only to Zone 8, consistently gives perhaps the finest foliage texture of any evergreen capable of completely covering the highest of brick walls. The small, narrow and dark leaflets are in pairs; what were once the terminal three have degenerated into three needle-pointed wiry claws which catch in mortar like steel hooks. With these the vine clambers easily up the tallest walls, and as easily over any shrubbery in its way. Although branching but sparsely, its multitude of stems and incorrigible vigor make up for the deficiency, since the stems swarm over each other and interweave to make a continuous cover. Rooted beneath azalea it is an especial menace, tougher than its competitor and more securely anchored. One may in desperation transplant and comb the roots of the outraged azalea, only to find that every cut fragment of *Doxantha* root and stem is cheerfully sending up new shoots. The golden flowers are of too brief duration to warrant its use in any but the most easily restricted situations.

Cherokee rose *(Rosa laevigata)* is often defended as the most valuable native rose in the southern states, so welcome and so fitting has it become to the landscape. High-climbing, rising to 40 feet or more, and conspicuous by its light green foliage at any time in summer, it is at its best when clothing a tree on the forest edge. In May, when dotted with its single white flowers nearly 4 inches across, it is a sight worth driving miles to see. (The name "Cherokee" is unfortunately often misapplied to another single-flowered rose—a Chinese adventurer, *Rosa bracteata,* which is not only far inferior in bloom but of a habit that has made it such a pest in grazing lands that its eradication has become a subject of considerable concern.)

Creeping Fig *(Ficus pumila)* is hardy only in the far South, for it withstands only a few degrees of frost. It is one of those Jekyll-and-Hyde plants that start out by matting a wall with diminutive, evergreen, deeply veined leaves so tender in appearance that it invites coddling. Abundantly able to care for itself when strongly rooted, it is capable of enveloping an entire building and raising upon it a forest of horizontal, coarse-leaved branches. These must be pruned away every year to preserve a trim effect. Although a single plant may go four or five stories high and cover 5000 square feet of wall, it is rather easily kept within bounds.

Kudzu *(Pueraria lobata),* native to China and Japan, and frequently hailed as the savior of the South's eroded lands, is not always an unmixed blessing. Its place

One of the most arresting and complex flowers a gardener is likely ever to see, passion-flower *(Passiflora incarnata)* is a common blue-flowered native in the South. A Brazilian relative is even larger and more colorful, with flowers four inches across.

is definitely in gullies and on sides of cutbanks and ravines. The difficulty is to make it stay there, for it travels underground as well as on the surface and is not easily controlled by any mechanical means. Our modern growth-regulating chemicals must be relied upon to keep it within bounds. Left to itself it could easily take the countryside, since it is not dismayed by trees 60 feet tall and often may be seen covering not only the clay banks where it was planted, but the face of the abutting forest as well.

Unusual Colors

Blue flowers among vines are somewhat rare. Two of the violet-toned nightshades, *Solanum rantonettii* and the much coarser and more lavender Costa Rican nightshade *(S. wendlandii)* offer welcome change from a surfeit of pink and white. Neither will withstand frost below 20°F., but both may be easily started from cuttings in a warm temperature.

Passion flower *(Passiflora incarnata)* is a common native throughout the South found abundantly rambling over fences and in waste places; it is too common to be much appreciated by many save those so divorced from country living that it seems to them a rare thing, an exotic. There are few flowers more remarkable in appearance or more intricately formed. The crown of colored filaments overlying the ten-parted floral envelope, the whole overtopped with three styles, and the five large-anthered stamens joined to make a supporting tube, all together make a most fantastic assemblage, 2 to 3 inches across.

Blue crown passion flower *(P. caerulea)*, a Brazilian, is even larger and showier, 4 inches across, with the rays blue, white, and purple. It is hardy about as far north as its native relative, that is, into Virginia. Other species or hybrids, either white or of various combinations of white, blue, purple, and red are mostly tender, lending their presence only to

Florida when unprotected. Some of these come satisfactorily (though not quickly) from seed, but all, apparently, strike well from cuttings of ripened wood. The little annual relative with yellow blossoms an inch across *(P. lutea)* is common over much of the same territory as *P. incarnata,* but it is little noticed and is seldom recognized as being a passion flower at all.

Less Hardy Vines

Evergreen wisteria *(Milletia megasperma),* from Australia, looks somewhat like the familiar oriental species of wisteria, though considerably coarser and darker because of the thick, evergreen leaves. The flowers appear somewhat later in the spring, and since the stems are never bare, are apt to be securely hidden from casual observation. The racemes are short and closely packed with small, dark reddish-purple flowers of a distinctive fragrance. Hardiness to only about 20°F. considerably restricts its range.

Another tender evergreen, the star-jasmine *(Trachelospermum jasminoides),* a Chinese acquisition, has been so long associated with the South that it has acquired the name of "Confederate," as though it were a native. The flowers are white, with a short tube and five twisted petals, and have an overpowering fragrance. Somewhat slow to start, after two or three years it becomes well rooted and will not only go to the house roof but will make such a heavy thatch of stems which accumulate leaves and bird nests, that it has to be continually reduced.

The farther one penetrates into the warmer portions of the South, those regions where freezing temperatures are less and less a limiting factor, the more spectacular are the flowers and flowering habits that come into view. Several vines are not fully hardy even along the Gulf Coast, which is subject to severe freezes now and then. They are commonly grown in that region, nonethless, on the gamble that they may survive several successive winters before a particularly severe cold spell destroys them. A series of warm winters promotes the extensive use of these tender species, only to be followed by discouragement when one or two cold nights (with temperatures below the mid-twenties) bring disaster. The discouragement is the more pronounced since the phenomenon occurs too rarely to accustom gardeners to losses and replacements any northern gardener would take as a matter of course. As a rule, plants are not protected, and their owners seem at a loss when faced with such emergencies.

The flowers of thunbergia *(T. grandiflora),* unlike those of its annual relative of northern gardens *(T. alata),* are large, and sky-blue on the wavy spreading border, nearly white in the throat. These flowers are borne in clusters of several to a dozen or more over a long period in midsummer, making a very beautiful display. The rather sandy, moist soil of the coastal region, with some leaf mold or rotted manure added,

Alamanda, a clambering evergreen viny shrub of frost-free climates. The handsome yellow trumpet-like flowers are up to five inches across.

George Taloumis

75

Buhle

seems to suit them well when the planting is made in light shade.

Two clerodendrums both called glorybower or bleeding-heart *(C. speciosum* and *C. thomsoniae)*, are hardy enough to be grown wherever the winters are rather mild, since both bloom on new wood, and usually are not severely damaged when cut to earth by frost. Both species have small, red, tubular flowers. They are borne in flat clusters 4 to 5 inches across. The red tube is nearly hidden by the inflated, 5-angled calyx, so only the spreading margin and stamens protrude. In *C. thomsoniae* this papery calyx is ivory-white, in the other dull pinkish. In both it is persistent for weeks after the red corolla has dropped away, giving an increasingly large display as blooming progresses, though the older clusters gradually decline in brilliance. The large, ovate, deeply-veined, dark green leaves alone are almost sufficient reason for growing these vines.

Allamanda *(A. cathartica)* is one of those questionables which make one wonder, each night of temperatures below freezing, whether or not they have been completely killed. It is obtainable in half a dozen varieties, robust or slender, large- or small-flowered; the smallest flowers are slightly larger than those of the northern trumpet vine, and the greatest, fully 5 inches across. The size and brilliance of these largest blossoms are quite staggering.

Most of the bougainvilleas are hardy only in areas completely free from frost, and in consequence are almost strictly confined (in the east) to Florida. The one exception is *B. glabra sanderiana.* This relatively hardy Brazilian is seen all along the Gulf Coast, where its massive color makes it an important addition to the sunny garden. It will not bloom well in shade. Cuttings of this variety root without difficulty over heat, and it sometimes sows itself. The less hardy species, red, orange, gold, scarlet, lavender, or white, root with more difficulty and are likely to be less free in their flowering.

Again, in bougainvillea it is not the corolla that gives the show, but the three large, brilliantly colored bracts, paper-thin and persistent. ✃

VINES FOR WINTER BEAUTY

A few vines give beauty the year round; these are well worth knowing

Donald Wyman

There are not many vines that have leaves or fruits all winter long, especially in northern gardens, so what few there are we should know well. First, of importance because it is grown from New England to Florida, is the English ivy *(Hedera helix),* a native of Europe but undoubtedly planted here in America since the earliest colonial times and now naturalizing itself in several places in the South..

At least seventy-five garden varieties of *Hedera helix* have been recognized by botanists recently and there are undoubtedly others. This is a considerably variable species, cultivated for centuries, probably one of the reasons why so many variants have been found. It is of interest to note that on old vines, the foliage of the branches on which appear the flowers and fruits, differs from the younger juvenile foliage. Cuttings taken of this older wood may be rooted (though less easily than juvenile portions), giving rise to shrubby plants, not at all like the vine which one customarily sees.

In the South, where this vine has been widely used and many old plants exist, the differences in the foliage on old and young portions of the vine are clearly present for all to see. In southern California, *Hedera* sp., especially *H. canariensis,* has been trained over wire fences and thus simulates excellent hedges. It withstands clipping well and of course functions as an evergreen hedge throughout the entire year. As a ground cover it hides rock piles or stone walls and covers trees and buildings.

A few varieties can be mentioned that show the different types available: 'Albany' is erect and shrubby in habit; 'Aureo-variegata' has leaves that are variegated with yellow, making this a truly beautiful specimen where it can be grown and displayed properly; 'Baltica,' one of the hardiest clones, apparently perfectly hardy in all but the most severe winters even in Boston; 'Conglomerata' with very small leaves, usually not over 1½ inches long and two-ranked on stiff upright stems, making it a popular and perky pot plant; 'Digitata' with leaves larger and five- to seven-lobed; 'Minima' with very small leaves but at the same time very unstable in habit; 'Pittsburgh' a variety in which lateral shoots appear in most of the leaf axils. These are only a few but will illustrate some of the variations available.

J. Horace McFarland

English ivy's dark, shiny, evergreen foliage is particularly welcome in winter when there is little else to catch and please the eye.

77

Creeping fig, an evergreen vine for the South and California, is particularly attractive when first filling in on a wall or building facade.

All in all *Hedera* is an excellent vine with many uses in the South as well as in the North and is one of the most common of all house plants also.

The only other truly evergreen vines in temperate regions are the various kinds of euonymus, mostly varieties of *E. fortunei,* which is itself a climber like the English ivy, attaching its small root-like holdfasts tenaciously to any upright with which it comes in contact. This native Chinese plant is also variable, and several varieties have arisen over the years. For a description of the principal varieties, see Lyle Blundell's article on page 53.

Honeysuckles

Two honeysuckles must be again mentioned in this grouping of vines for winter beauty, namely, Hall's honeysuckle (*Lonicera japonica* 'Halliana') which has been thoroughly described elsewhere in these articles, and Henry honeysuckle *(L. henryi)* which is slightly more hardy and not as rampant a grower. Both have evergreen foliage except near the extreme limit of their range. (Boston, northern New York, and Ohio) and are adaptable as either ground covers or twining vines.

Bittersweets

The bittersweets certainly must be mentioned, for, although there are other fruiting vines some of which hold their fruits long into fall, these hold their fruits far into the winter or until such time as the birds eat them. Two species are commonly grown, the native American bittersweet *(Celastrus scandens)* and the oriental bittersweet *(C. orbiculata).* In both the sexes are separate as is explained elsewhere, and in both the winter beauty is provided by the bright colored orange and red fruits.

The difference between these two species is that in the American bittersweet the fruits are borne in terminal clusters of many berries, while in the oriental bittersweet the fruits are borne in small lateral clusters. The leaves of the latter are also more rounded or orbicular than are those of the American native. The oriental species is especially robust and has become naturalized in much of the eastern United States.

In the South

The farther south one goes, the more evergreen vines one finds in the gardens. South of Washington, D.C., for instance, in addition to the vines already mentioned, the twining scarlet kadsura *(Kadsura japonica)* begins to appear here and there in gardens. It is of value for its evergreen foliage, scarlet berries, and reddish autumn color. A few of the more protected gardens are fortunate in growing the blue crown passion flower *(Passiflora caerulea)* with semi-evergreen leaves, climbing by tendrils and with beautiful blue to pure white flowers, one of the most beautiful of the passion flowers that can be grown in this country. One of the best evergreen climbers for this particular area is *Pileostegia viburnoides* with its excellent glossy green leaves, and a growing habit similar to that of the climbing hydrangea.

A little farther south the Himalayan magnolia-vine *(Schisandra propinqua)* can be used. An evergreen vine with orange flowers and brilliant red berries, unfortunately it is in that group of plants which have all the staminate flowers on one plant and the fruiting or pistillate flowers on another. The catclaw funnel creeper *(Macfadyena unguis-cati)* also is a popular evergreen.

From Charleston, South Carolina, south into even warmer climates, other evergreen vines are used, such as the beautiful purple-bell cobaea *(Cobaea scandens)*. Sometimes called cup-and-saucer vine, it has 2-inch-long bell-shaped flowers of lavender to purple, tenacious tendrils, and the excellent characteristic of blooming during a six month period. The creeping fig *(Ficus pumila)* should certainly not be overlooked, for as a closely attached small-leaved evergreen vine on a wall it really has no peers. In fact, the stems hold themselves so tightly to the wall, that when they cross each other they frequently become grafted together. The young growth of this vine is what is mostly desired for it forms the perfect closely knit wall covering.

These are a few of the vines of interest during winter. Though those which can be grown in the far South are more numerous and varied in character than the species available in the North, all can add a bit of cheerfulness to any garden where they prove hardy. ✄

Dishcloth Gourd

The dishcloth gourd, also called vegetable sponge, is an interesting curiosity, used to some extent commercially. The long slender fruit has a fibrous interior that furnishes a satisfactory sponge-like material when it is dried and the seeds are removed. In some parts of the world young fruits are eaten as a vegetable. The fruit itself is not as colorful as are most gourds, but the yellow flowers, which may be five inches across, are quite showy. The vine makes a useful late summer screen.

There are several species, *Luffa aegyptiaca* being the most commonly grown. It can be grown in the northern United States, but needs a long growing season to fruit abundantly. The plants are not demanding, but like full sun. Culture is much the same as for cucumber or melons. Good for pot scrubbing or in the bath for dry skin spots. ✄

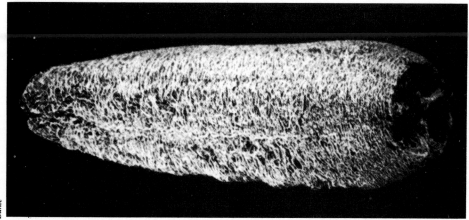

Buhle

THE WORLD'S MOST EXTENSIVE
GARDENING BOOK SERIES

EACH PUBLICATION a complete, concise, well-illustrated manual of 64 to 104 pages, with ideas to put to work in any garden. (These Handbooks are separate editions of special-feature issues of PLANTS & GARDENS.) One of America's best horticultural values. Arranged by subject:

For latest brochure send us a postcard: Brooklyn Botanic Garden, 1000 Washington Ave., Brooklyn, NY 11225.